The Royal Institution

Also by Gwendy Caroe

WILLIAM HENRY BRAGG: MAN AND SCIENTIST
Cambridge University Press

TOUCHING BEAUTY'S HAND:
AN ILLUSTRATED ANTHOLOGY OF PROSE AND VERSE
privately published

The Royal Institution

AN INFORMAL HISTORY

Gwendy Caroe

with a final chapter by Alban Caroe

John Murray

FIFTY ALBEMARLE STREET

First published 1985
by John Murray (Publishers) Ltd
50 Albemarle Street, London W1X 4BD

Typeset by Inforum Ltd, Portsmouth
Printed and bound in Great Britain
by Butler & Tanner Ltd, Frome

British Library CIP Data
Caroe, Gwendy
The royal institution : an informal history.
1. Royal Institution of Great Britain——History
I. Title
506'.041   Q41.R88
ISBN 0–7195–4245–6

Contents

Illustrations

The line drawings on pages xii, 42, and 120 are by the author.

Preface

THERE WAS an abnormal break in the writing of this book caused by my wife's death, and some explanation is required as to how much of it is her own work and how much has been added later.

When she died suddenly in 1982 the first three chapters were in typescript, and her manuscripts of Chapters 4 and 5 (Tyndall and Dewar) had been brought to the point at which she was satisfied that their texts could be submitted to the expert scientists and historians whose advice she valued so highly. Chapter 6 (which she thought of as 'us') had virtually reached the same stage after she had pencilled in some important additions during the last week of her life. Chapters 7 and 8 (Lectures and Education) had been written out a couple of months earlier but were also due for revision. During the next six months and following her intentions all these chapters were submitted for criticism to 'experts' chosen under authoritative advice, and have later been amended and edited to embody their suggestions, many expressed in enthusiastic terms. So many of them, however, stated that she had cut Chapter 6 far too short that I felt justified in enlarging it by taking in three extracts from the talk she gave to the Library Circle on 15 March 1965, which had won repeated praise from her brother W.L. Bragg who was present. But I have set my face against any attempts to invent further comments which she might have added to her text in response to pressure for more.

She had deliberately refrained from starting any drafts for the final chapter, meaning to wait until she had been fortified by expert guidance on what had gone before. When she last discussed that chapter with me she was still intending to hasten her narrative to its conclusion with increasing speed. She has explained some of her reasons for such thinking on page 106 which I have left unaltered, but I have no doubt that she would have changed her view if she had lived to read the cumulative advice of 'the experts'. Every one of those who read her later chapters urged that her treatment of developments at the RI ought not to culminate in anticlimax. The problems which face Science and

Society are as great today as they have ever been, and any interest which her story may arouse should be brought up to date and ought not to fade away fifteen years ago. She would have accepted this verdict; and she would certainly have gone back to 'the experts' for further guidance. I tried therefore to follow as closely as possible in the footsteps I believed she would have trod, and it was at first agreed that the last chapter should be written by Sir Gordon Cox. Temporary ill-health unfortunately made that impossible, and I eventually took the task on myself, with much help. I thought it right to enlarge that chapter to include a few additional points which might have been placed chronologically in Chapter 6.

This book has thus been greatly helped by contributions from many persons, and she wanted full acknowledgements to be made if ever it saw the light of day. I must start by passing on some of the gratitude which I know was already brimming over in her mind while she was still at work. Such thoughts of hers went first to Mrs Irene McCabe, Librarian at the RI, who had searched out information so frequently and passed it on with so much understanding that ties of real affection were formed between them. Second she would have placed Sir Gordon Cox who read through her drafts at many stages with the same critical but also constructive approach as he had already given to her earlier biography of her father Sir William Bragg; not only helping her to avoid mistakes but also contributing important suggestions. Amongst many others who helped to open new windows for her in her search for insight she would have mentioned Mrs Sophie Forgan.

Next she would have wished me to acknowledge with gratitude the trouble taken by various 'experts' who were good enough to read through and comment upon the typescripts of her chapters which I sent out posthumously to persons whom Sir George Porter had recommended. Amongst these I would specially mention Dr W.H. Brock, Mrs Margaret Gray, Sir David Phillips, Professor J.S. Rowlinson, Professor C.A. Russell and Professor C.A. Taylor. The suggestions of all these have been worked in wherever possible, though I have tried to retain as much of her original phraseology as I could.

Thirdly I have thanks of my own to give in connection with the last chapter. Though Sir Gordon Cox could not write it himself, he continued to support me with the same invaluable advice as he had earlier given to my wife. I could not have undertaken the task without

Sir George Porter's encouragement, supplemented by the large collection of relevant documents which Miss Judith Wright sorted out for me on his instructions; and I recall the joy with which I listened to Bill Coates's vivid answers to my many questions about experimental lecturing. Professor Ronald King made some particularly helpful comments on several points. Yet, despite all this help I must stress that I alone am responsible for all shortcomings in the final text of Chapter 9.

And there are others to whom I must also say thank you: to Mrs McCabe again for unstinted help with the illustrations and the lists of sources and suggestions for further reading; to Mrs Margaret Gray for compiling the index; to my publishers for having allotted to me such a sympathetic and at the same time constructive editor in Mr Roger Hudson; and last but not least to Mr and Mrs George Pretty who together typed all chapters in this book, thus providing a fitting culmination to the support which I and my family have been receiving from him for over fifty years.

I salute them all.

A.D.R. Caroe
July 1985

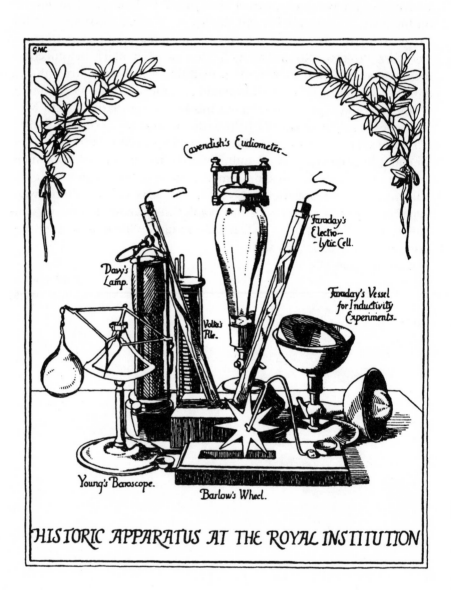

Cavendish's Eudiometer.

Faraday's Electro-lytic Cell.

Davy's Lamp.

Faraday's Vessel for Inductivity Experiments.

Volta's Pile.

Young's Baroscope.

Barlow's Wheel.

HISTORIC APPARATUS AT THE ROYAL INSTITUTION

ONE

Background and Founding
of the Royal Institution

COUNT RUMFORD

I N MARCH 1799 a group of prominent men were invited to a
meeting at No. 32 Soho Square London, the home of Sir Joseph
Banks, President of the Royal Society. The group included one
Duke, six Earls, many Lords, the Prince-Bishop of Durham, sixteen
Members of Parliament, two Directors of the Bank of England, an
ex-Lord Mayor of London and Mr William Wilberforce; also Mr
Thomas Bernard, a dedicated philanthropist, and one extraordinary
ex-American. They represented the cream of London's aristocratic
society and they were met to create a new Institution. As science was to
be its inspiration, it was natural that the meeting should be chaired by
Sir Joseph Banks, for he was the corner-stone of English science with an
international reputation.

The object of the new Institution would be philanthropic; it was to
harness science to the job of improving the lot of the poor. Everyone
accepted that there must always be 'the poor', and they were very
necessary to those who were not poor. The very culture and leisure of
these gentlemen gathered together that March day depended on the
poor, on a large work force to maintain their estates and man the
expanding industry of England.

The poor were in a particularly bad way at the end of the 18th
century, unsettled to danger point and hungry. England was at war
with France and food prices had soared. Life in much of the country had
changed as agricultural methods were improved, common rights were
lost and cottage industry dwindled. There followed a drift to the towns
in search of work and better wages. In many cases the result was that
the 'rural' poor became an urban poor, perhaps with more money but
with uncertainty and a bewildering loneliness, cut off from the hard but
homely contacts of village life. Too often the next generation in the
towns knew nothing but terrible conditions; they could easily be roused

to a riot for a bit of fun or chance of loot. Mob violence was a prevalent fear for the comfortable middle class, there being no police to control times of tension (a town had but one or two constables), and the French mob had shown what mobs could do. Many thinking people were deeply troubled about the situation, coupled with some anxiety for the stability of England and concern for their own way of life. Landowning aristocrats were prominent among such people.

The gentlemen who met in Soho Square that March afternoon represented the Church, Society and Science united in a common aim, which was to put into effect a philanthropic scheme suggested by the strange ex-American, Benjamin Thompson, Count Rumford. Something of an adventurer, brilliant and devious, he had published some essays on social subjects in the mid 1790s, and they had roused considerable interest. His 1796 essay contained a sketch of a possible scientific–philanthropic Institution where science would be used to help, inform and improve the condition of the poor. Jeremy Bentham had expressed enthusiasm for these ideas.

Thomas Bernard, a wealthy and almost professional philanthropist, was also enthused and with his friends had formed a society to consider Rumford's suggestions; it was called 'the Society for Bettering the Condition and Increasing the Comforts of the Poor', or the 'Bettering Society' as it was called for short. They discussed what might be done and they made Rumford a member of the Society. Rumford wrote to thank Bernard, 'Go on, my dear Sir, and be assured that when you shall have put *doing good* into fashion, you will have done all that human wisdom can do to retard and prolong the decline of a great and powerful nation that has arrived at, or passed, the zenith of human glory.' (England was suffering a sense of failure from the recent loss of her American colonies.)

Early in 1799 a committee of members of the Bettering Society met Rumford to hear more about his scheme for an Institution; those gathered in March at Banks's house were there to implement a revised version of it. Rumford had set out his ideas as:

The Proposals for forming by subscription in the Metropolis of the British Empire a Public Institution for diffusing the knowledge and facilitating the general introduction of useful mechanical invention and improvements, and for teaching by courses of philosophical lectures and experiments the application of science to the common purposes of life.

Science (then normally called natural philosophy) was to be used for social welfare, in an attempt to tuck in again the loosened roots of the working class. If the poor were better equipped and better informed, would they not have greater respect for their betters and be more content with their station in a traditional hierarchy? Order was all important, order in society and public order. After the events in France everybody was frightened of change, upper class and work people alike, and movements for reform which had been gathering strength through the 18th century were halted.

Each of the gentlemen gathered at Banks's house had declared himself willing to put down at least fifty guineas to start the new venture. Though Rumford had called it a 'Public Institution' it was to be privately owned and administered; the subscribing gentlemen, fifty to start with and soon many more, would be the 'Proprietors' and they would elect a governing body to run *their* Institution.

The Earl of Winchilsea was proposed as the first President. The Managers (there were to be nine altogether) would of course include Rumford, Bernard and Banks, who was a great landlord, breeding sheep as well as being President of the Royal Society; also Lord Spencer who had vast estates and the finest private library in Europe, and Lord Egremont of Petworth. Petworth House was nicknamed a 'college for agriculture', its interiors and the view from its windows were painted by Turner. Another Manager was the Earl of Chichester whose seat was at Stanmer under the South Downs. Among the Proprietors were Sir John Coxe Hippisley, Vice President of the West of England Agricultural Society, and Lord Palmerston, who owned Broadlands near Romsey. The Duke of Devonshire was probably the grandest and the Prince-Bishop of Durham possibly the richest, with vast acres and coal mines, but he was a great philanthropist too.

Most of the Proprietors were 'improving landlords'. Following 'Turnip Townshend', a pioneer with his rotation of crops, and Coke of Holkham, manuring his light soils in Norfolk and turning his sandy wastes into money, these big landowners had made the enclosures about which the village folk were so bitter. But how could they have practised the new methods, improved their breeds of sheep and cattle, used the new seed drilling machinery, planted their rotations, without enclosing land? Indeed it was inevitable and right that the new ways should spread; the rising population of England had to be fed somehow.

To study the agricultural problems on their estates the 'improving landlords' had set up a private society which they called the Board of Agriculture in 1793. To study the social problems of their work force many of them became members of the Bettering Society in 1796, and now offered themselves as Proprietors of the new Institution. Their interest in problems social, scientific and agricultural marched together.

These landowners were the great Whig Lords who had virtually run England in the 18th century. They spent the greater part of the year on their country estates, and came to Town for the parliamentary session, trundling up uncomfortably in their heavy coaches in the earlier part of the century; in the latter part they felt themselves speeding to London on the new turnpike roads. This ruling Society was made up of only about three or four hundred families, operating within a network of patronage. Place was obtained by support, solicited or bought or owned. To get elected to Parliament cost more and more as the century advanced. But Parliament was only the most glaring example of place-seeking and dealing. To gain advancement in State or Church it was necessary to have the right politics and influential friends. Wealthy, living in one or more country palaces, the great landlord was hardly touched by the new industrialism, though he had woken up to the profit to be got from developing his coal mines or digging canals like the Duke of Bridgwater, so that Durham coal or Wedgwood pottery could glide cheaply and safely to port and city. A rising tide of new middle-class radicalism might criticise this oligarchy in the latter years of the century, but the oligarchy still needed courting.

Power made these people at the top the leaders of taste and fashion. The word 'fashion' had a more distinguished meaning then than it has now, when it may only be something in a shop window or a glossy magazine. At the end of the 18th century it meant the lead in appreci-ation of art and literature, in music and thought, as well as in dress and manners. These oligarchs were the people on whose backing the new Institution would rely and it is interesting to note how often the word 'fashion' appears in the early records. To attract Fashion, meaning the leaders of fashion, was essential to the Institution's survival and growth.

Apart from Banks himself there is in the list of the original Proprietors only one representative of pure science, Henry Cavendish. It is true that he was very rich and the grandson of a Duke of Devonshire, but one wonders if he was seeing possibilities of real scientific development within the new venture.

Another famous name in the list is that of William Wilberforce. He was on the Bettering Society committee that met Rumford in January 1799. It was probably he who brought in his friends Samuel and Henry Thornton, both bankers and Members of Parliament. Henry was a director of the Bank of England and lived in a large house on Clapham Common. For some years Wilberforce lived there with him and the Thornton home became a meeting place for Wilberforce's supporters. Wilberforce and the Thorntons were free from the landowning self-interest of so many of the other Proprietors; they represented Philanthropy, but with a special slant. They belonged to what was dubbed the 'Clapham Sect' and practised philanthropy in the new spirit of concern that had been growing during the latter half of the 18th century. The Wesleys had lit a fire and the evangelical spirit was spreading inside and outside the Established Church, up and down and through society. By Victoria's day it would reach the top. The Clapham Sect ('the Saints') upheld the evangelical gospel of thrift and a godly Sabbath; they were good people but somewhat narrow, with little sympathy for idleness or drink. The poor did not always care for them. The early warmth was dying out of Methodism; work and get on was becoming too much its creed, with self-satisfaction replacing joy.

All these 'philanthropists' of the Bettering Society had been thinking, searching for solutions, especially a solution for the problems of the rural areas. This was natural considering that the thinkers were mainly country landlords. It would be some time yet before attention was given to the urban poor. Providing allotments was one scheme put forward, three acres and a cow for each rural worker; another scheme was to provide research into the improving of cottage industries, such as spinning, weaving and tanning. There was a harvest of good-will available, ripe and ready and anxious; eager to help the poor, anxious to stabilize an order that seemed to be rocking. Moreover, Church, State and Society were all on the same side; there was no anti-clericalism to divide England in the 18th century, as there was in France. The gentlemen of the Bettering Society were impressed by the new tool of applied science which had done so much for Industry in the north. Rumford's suggestions were the match to the well-laid fire; without the anxious good-will waiting ready, his schemes might have remained on paper or fizzled out.

There are two men who stand out among the Proprietors as most important in supporting Rumford at the birth of the new Institution:

Bernard, perhaps the most compassionate man of them all, the actual founder of the Bettering Society; and Banks, the most weighty figure, representing science.

Thomas Bernard, heir to a baronetcy, was a wealthy barrister who had retired early to devote himself to philanthropy. He had started a School for the Indigent Blind, a Society for the relief of Poor Neighbours in Distress, the London Fever Hospital, the Cancer Institution, and an Institute for the Protection and Instruction of Climbing Boys. A family needed every penny when times were bad in London's wildly fluctuating labour market; the children of the poor were put to work as soon as they could be used, and young boys were the right size for climbing the chimneys of those days. Bernard's chief occupation in the 1790s was as Treasurer of the Foundling Hospital, established in 1740 and still full of unwanted babies in his day. Bernard, acquainted with Rumford's writings, wrote to consult him about practical problems at the Hospital. Rumford was delighted to advise on the re-organisation of the kitchens which resulted in considerable saving of fuel, and won Bernard's confidence in his ingenious ability.

Bernard knew Rumford in a scientifically domestic capacity; Sir Joseph Banks knew him as a Fellow of the Royal Society and a natural philosopher who had made valuable contributions to pure science. Banks was for forty-one years President of the Royal Society. A distinguished botanist, born of a wealthy family, he had sailed with Captain Cook on his first voyage in 1768, providing at his own expense the staff and equipment for collection of botanical specimens and study of natural history. Under Banks the Royal Society had acquired an international reputation and he entertained and corresponded with foreign scientists. When Humboldt, travelling in South America while France was at war with England, wanted to get his archaeological collection safely back to Europe, he, a French citizen, consigned it to Sir Joseph in England. Sir Joseph backed many scientific projects and if he is criticized for admitting as Fellows to the Society too many who were distinguished less for science than by their social or other eminence, one must remember it was a time for the lordly amateur. The new Institution would court these same people.

Banks and Bernard had every confidence in Rumford; the Proprietors were enthusiastic. At the historic meeting on 7 March 1799 the Institution was formally founded. Petition was made to the King for a Charter, and in the following year the Institution became the 'Royal

Institution of Great Britain' – the 'RI', as members have called it and as I shall usually call it as I proceed with its story.

But who after all was Rumford? It is time to tell something of him. Really an extraordinary man, Rumford had been a soldier, was a scientist, and above all had an abiding passion for organisation. Only some sketch of his life can explain and illustrate his ideas.

Rumford, Count of the Holy Roman Empire, was born Benjamin Thompson in the State of Massachusetts (he took his title from a township on the border of Massachusetts and New Hampshire). Of humble parentage, he grew up in the years of discontent under the insensitive British administration. Through marriage at nineteen with a rich widow he became one of the Governor's 'set' amidst the suspicion and jealousy of the local population. War breaking out, he made himself useful collecting information for the King's forces, was sent back to England with despatches for the Colonial Secretary, and remained in London as his protégé and expert adviser on the New England colonies. He rose to be Under Secretary of State for the Colonies. But when the Government was likely to fall he quickly returned to America as colonel of a regiment he was to raise there, the King's American Dragoons; after sixteen months the Peace brought him home. Retired now on full pay he proposed to travel and make his 'Grand Tour' on the Continent and, 'If there be a war I shall engage in it, on one side or the other. I don't care a farthing which!'

Thompson, aged thirty, had learned to manipulate the world he moved in; when he manoeuvred for office and advantage he incurred distrust, but when there was something active to be done he compelled admiration for his energy and cleverness. As he wandered across Europe he continued his service to the British Government as an intelligence agent; arrived in Munich he met and charmed the Elector, took service with him and stayed. A useful man to have at the Bavarian Court, George III conferred a knighthood on him, though in actual fact Sir Benjamin did less and less for Britain as he became totally involved in Bavarian affairs. In the Elector's service he found infinite possibilities for his administrative skill, as things were in a bad state. He reorganised the Bavarian army, re-clothed it according to his own design, the uniforms made in his 'Military Workhouse', and he built a 'House of Industry' for the swarming beggars in Munich, sending the military one day to round them all up. He made financial profit out of their industry, feeding the workers in his scientifically designed soup kitchens and warming them with his fuel-saving stoves.

It was all an enormous success which the Elector recognised by creating Sir Benjamin Count of the Holy Roman Empire; Rumford had proved himself to be a brilliant organizer. He was also a philanthropist, but, one feels, a cold one, more interested in the means and efficiency of his philanthropy than the people he was aiming to help. Their need was his opportunity to put his theories into practice.

His theories were very clever, his inventions brilliant examples of applied science; for Rumford was also a distinguished natural philosopher, his scientific research taking shape from the problems under his hand. War had been his occupation, so he studied cannon and the heat produced in boring them. For a paper on gunpowder (ninety-nine pages long) he had been elected a Fellow of the Royal Society in 1780; for his work on heat insulation (he had clothed an army and established that it is the air trapped in fur or cloth that is the key to its insulating capacity) the Royal Society later gave him its Copley Medal. In the meantime he had designed a frigate. Heat and dynamics are the scientific subjects for which he is remembered with respect.

A quotation from his writing shows his fascination with the application of scientific technology to social problems.

Having long been in a habit of considering all useful improvements as being purely *mechanical*, or as depending on the perfection of machinery and address in the management of it, and of considering *profit* (which depends much on the perfection of machinery) as the only incitement to *industry*, I was naturally led to meditate on the means that might be employed with advantage to diffuse the knowledge and facilitate the general introduction of such improvements.

A shrewd if chilly statement; but the hearts of the English philanthropists could use such a head.

Rumford's first idea which had inspired the founding of the Bettering Society had been to set up public kitchens and workhouses to provide food and useful employment for the poor of London on the Munich model. On to this he then had grafted further ideas for an exhibition centre of 'useful mechanical improvements', and had changed his scheme from feeding the poor to instructing artisans. In his Institution 'philosophers' would investigate in order to invent new improvements, workmen would be taught how to use them, and the gentry would come to support with their patronage and interest. He hoped that the Institution would become a guiding inspiration for many establishments in other centres. Indeed the Count persuaded his particular friend Lady Palmerston to start a private 'School of Industry' on the Broadlands estate, near Romsey.

The Bettering Society had hesitated over Rumford's ambitious development of his earlier ideas, but now in March 1799 he easily raised enough money and enthusiasm to push his scheme through. He was proud of the list of lordly backers, but perhaps Bernard realised the more clearly how much these would have to be catered for: a club for the rich would have to be combined with the interests of the poor.

Rumford laid special emphasis on the proposed exhibition of models of improved types of trade and domestic appliances. They would include 'cottage fireplaces, kitchen utensils for a cottage for the family of a gentleman of fortune, a complete laundry, economical grates [with fires burning in them in the cold season], and there would be spinning wheels and looms for the use of the poor – together with such other machinery as may be useful in giving them employment at home', which was just what the landowners wanted. But there were also to be models of bridges and lime kilns and ventilators, and 'It is likewise proposed to exhibit *working models*, on a reduced scale, of that most curious and most useful machine, the steam engine'.

For 'teaching the application of science to the useful purposes of life' a lecture room was to be fitted up and also a 'complete laboratory with philosophical apparatus'. Rumford listed a number of subjects suitable for lectures such as 'Heat and its use', 'of the methods of procuring and preserving ice in summer', and of preserving food, of cooling liquors, of bleaching, of tanning, of soap making, dyeing, of vegetation and manures. It is noticeable how many of these subjects are apposite to the landowning interest and country house life, but he does end with 'all mechanical arts'.

There followed in Rumford's proposals a long piece on the organization and financing of the Institution. Its situation was most important; it would have to be in a place convenient for the fashionable world. A large house was acquired in Albemarle Street in the new residential quarter of Mayfair, an easy stroll from the clubs of St James's, close to the shops of Bond Street and not too far from Westminster for the eighteen Members of Parliament among the original Proprietors.

There seemed to be no worry about finance at the beginning; within a few months the Institution could list 132 Proprietors and a large number of life and annual subscribers. Fashion had rallied to the call, and with £8000 capital Rumford started enthusiastically on converting 21 Albemarle Street with the help of Thomas Webster, a young architectural student whom he made Clerk of the Works. Rumford had enormous fun, organized everything and everybody to his own will, and with brilliant drive and hustle began to get 'his' Institution under way.

No. 21 Albemarle Street was a gracious house with a dividing staircase in a wide entrance hall. This was the main entrance until 1928 and the hall and staircase remain intact, though the front door has been moved. Society could mount the stairs with dignity to reach the fine room on the first floor which would become the Library, though at first it had to be used for lectures; the room below was and still is styled the 'Conversation Room'. In fact, the best rooms at No. 21 were to be arranged for the reception of Fashion from the start; it soon became the scientific club of aristocratic London.

A room at the back of the ground floor was set aside as the 'Repository' for the exhibition of models on which Rumford set so much store. At first it was furnished with his own cooking pots and stoves (another of his special stoves was installed in the Managers' Room; alas it has been swept away, but I remember it). The 'Rumford Grate' was on show and became well known; Jane Austen describes General Tilney standing in front of his Rumford Grate at Northanger Abbey. Some agricultural machinery was exhibited, lent by landowners; but when application was made to industrial firms to send models of their latest machines, Rumford ran into unexpected difficulty. Manufacturers did not want to lend machinery; they were fearful of trade secrets being disclosed. Matthew Boulton, a prominent industrialist, wrote to Rumford:

Your object is one that every practical inventor should discountenance . . . Suppose a man, by a great devotion of time and labour, by skill and ingenuity, has made an important combination in chemistry and mechanics, your object is to publish the details of his labour, to enable every spectator to profit by his knowledge. This . . . would be ruinous to individuals and would ultimately interfere with the prosperity of Britain, for your enemies would profit by such disclosure . . .

Patent law gave very limited protection, it was little changed from the days of monopolies and would not be revised until the 1860s.

The manufacturers' refusal of support was a big blow to Rumford. He had believed that 'An Institution of this nature is peculiarly calculated to produce that unity of pursuit between manufacturers and men of science which is absolutely necessary for obtaining perfection in the theory as well as in the practice of all the arts of civilized life.'

Rumford's was a Baconian ideology of the marriage between science and the arts for the benefit of mankind, meaning by 'the arts', not fine arts, or what we today just call 'art', but the arts of doing this or making that, from baking bread, a domestic art, to the art of weaving cloth or building bridges. In the new industrial age, Rumford had such hopes of the co-operation of the man of science and the industrialist. In his Prospectus he had set out the reciprocal position of the 'philosopher' and the manufacturer:

It is the business of these philosophers to examine every operation of nature or of art, and to establish general theories for the direction and conducting of future processes. Invention seems to be peculiarly the province of the man of science; his ardour in the spirit of truth is unremitted; discovery is his harvest; utility his reward. Yet it may be demanded whether his moral and intellectual habits are precisely such as may be calculated to produce useful practical improvements. Detached as he usually is from the ordinary pursuits of life, little if at all accustomed to contemplate the scheme of profit and loss – will he descend from the sublime general theories of science and enter into the details of weight, measure, price, quality? – Are his motives and his powers equal to this task? Surely they are not. The practical knowledge – the stimulus of interest – and the capital of the manufacturer are here wanting, while the manufacturer on his part, is equally in want of the general information and accurate reasoning of the man of science.

It was a foreshadowing of the advantage of organised industrial research, more than a century before the Department of Scientific and Industrial Research was founded in 1916, and even then it would be another ten years or so before industry fully realised the help that science could provide. In 1800 it was out of the question for even a scientifically inclined manufacturer like Boulton to have his newly invented machinery displayed in Albemarle Street.

So Rumford's Repository, or model room, remained rather under-furnished, save for his own inventions. However, a kitchen was equipped and a room prepared where the Managers might give dinners to show off the food cooked in Rumford's pots on his 'kitchen range'. In a modern book on French chefs Rumford is lauded as the inventor of the kitchen range which saved cooks from the intolerable heat of the old methods of spit-roasting before wide-fronted open grates, such as one sees in the Pavilion at Brighton and in many old college and country-house kitchens of the 18th century. His 'range' meant also a great saving in fuel.

Then there was the laboratory. Rumford had specified an 'airy and well lit laboratory' which would be used for preparing demonstrations for lectures and also for making special investigations. Rumford and the Managers considered bread-making, food for cattle, 'fire balls and combustible cakes', and iron founding to be suitable subjects for study. Pure scientific research which would later bring fame to the R I was not in Rumford's plan, which stopped short at 'investigations'. In his Institution, science was primarily intended to make itself useful.

This was very much the emphasis at that time. It had been the other way round a hundred years or so before. Science put to use, as recommended by Bacon, and Newton's pure science exist naturally side by side, but sometimes the balance of interest has been on one side, sometimes on the other. Experimental science had begun to flower during the mess of the Civil Wars; Charles II had set his seal on it at the foundation of the Royal Society in 1662; Newton's *Principia* and his piety had given weight and dignity to it. The early Fellows of the RS were like children let out into scientific fields to play and search for strange things with excited curiosity – and curiosity is the spirit of pure science. The satirists of the 18th century laughed at the early Fellows for their impracticability; but they read their scientific writings and paid their philosophers the compliment of notice, lampooning them with wicked wit. Swift describes Gulliver on his Travels visiting the Academy of Lagado, where the philosophers were busy making sunshine out of cucumbers, the Academy, of course, being the Royal Society.

That first quick flowering of experimental science naturally faded, and the 18th century became a period of tidying up and sorting the seed. But there were some great natural philosophers. The eccentric Cavendish (1731–1810) made highly important contributions to science by his work on the isolation and identification of gases, and on the nature of electricity; but he considered his discoveries to be his own private property and did not always bother to communicate them, even to the Royal Society. Faraday had to re-discover many of Cavendish's findings. Priestley (1733–1804) made important discoveries about oxygen and other gases, and while so doing established methods of experimental investigation which became normal practice among chemical researchers. He also helped to undermine the old theory of Phlogiston, thought to be the essential element in combustion, although he was loath to believe his own results. It was left to Lavoisier, the great French chemist, to order Priestley's results and postulate a new theory of 'caloric' which was in turn questioned by both Rumford and Humphry Davy. However, science was an extra for Priestley; he considered his life-work to be in theology and philosophy. He was a notorious radical, supporting the American and French revolutionaries. Dr Johnson thundered at him and a mob wrecked his laboratory in Birmingham.

For his natural history and botanical work Sir Joseph Banks must also be classed with the followers of pure science; but as an agriculturalist he was very ready to apply science, and employ it to improve his estates.

One reason for the intelligent interest taken in science in the 18th century was that the gentleman amateur could understand scientific writing; whether ridiculed or appreciated, it was *read*, for it was written in his own language, in ordinary educated English. As yet there was little need of specialised words, and divisive jargon was two centuries away into the future. Moreover the cultured man was helped by knowing some science anyway; it was part of the comprehensive education he aimed at acquiring. He would take pride in possessing a few scientific instruments. George III had a fine collection.

The 18th century had intellectual ideals. Itinerant lecturers toured the country, speaking in halls or private houses or, towards the end of the century, at one of the Literary and Philosophical Societies that were springing up on the pattern of the Manchester 'Lit and Phil' founded in 1781. Science lectures were popular, especially chemistry lectures (elementary chemistry is fun: chemistry sets are sold in toy-shops today). These gentlemen who were so interested we now call 'amateurs of science'; but one must remember that at that time there were no 'professionals' – science was an extension of knowledge, and those who were devoted to it and experimented in it worked from the niche of an established profession, usually that of a physician, unless they had private means, like Cavendish or Banks.

This aspect of 'useful' science had been growing to prominence during the second half of the 18th century, as evidenced as early as 1754 by the foundation of the society now known as The Royal Society of Arts whose initial objectives were to distribute 'premiums for the promoting of improvements in the liberal arts and sciences, manufactures, etc'. The main aim was to increase not only the number but also the skills of craftsmen of all kinds. Response was dramatic and was boosted by the spread of the Industrial Revolution. Industrial inventiveness had roped in science, and science had stimulated invention; the itinerant lecturers such as amused and interested the gentry were to be found in large numbers in the industrial north as they toured to teach some science to the men in charge of the machines. The late 18th century saw the rise of technology; pure science seemed in danger of being harnessed and Rumford's Institution illustrated the trend.

This brings us back to the building problems of the Royal Institution in its first year, since a lecture theatre had to be built for the 'philosophical lectures' that were to be given. The plans and general set-up of another institution must have been known to Rumford – namely Anderson's Institution in Glasgow, founded in 1796 to serve the interest in technical science in Scotland. Its aims were akin to Rumford's for the RI, and the reputation of its Professor and the excellence of its lecture theatre were such that Rumford enticed away the Professor, Dr Garnett, and copied aspects of Anderson's for his own theatre in Albemarle Street. There was a vacant lot (old gardens) to the north of No. 21 and the RI lecture theatre was constructed partly over it. To this day it is accounted one of the best scientific lecture theatres ever planned for sight and acoustics.

Thomas Webster, Clerk of the Works, was in charge of the construction, though the careful Managers got in a couple of architects to advise and check his plans, John Soane and George Saunders who worked on the British Museum. This must have been galling for Webster, but Rumford backed him. Webster constructed a stone staircase leading directly from the street to the gallery in the theatre. The gallery was for the artisans, to segregate them from their employers who might be sitting below, and so save embarrassment for both. The Institution had opened its doors in 1800; within two years the theatre was ready. How so much got done in such a short space of time remains a miracle, a feat due to Rumford's drive and autocratic direction. And how the money stretched to so much building is a miracle too. Rumford spent and spent; Bernard the Treasurer watched funds and the Proprietors, dazzled by Rumford but trusting Bernard, put their hands into their long pockets again and again. And wise old Sir Joseph Banks was still behind the enterprise.

Webster also had ideas of his own for the RI. As Clerk of the Works he had experienced difficulty with uneducated workmen who could not follow his instructions. He was enthusiastic to start a school for artisans; indeed it was the hope of making such a school that had induced him to take service in Albemarle Street. Rumford approved his ideas as they chimed with his own. The scheme was that workmen should be released from their country jobs to come up to London and board at the Institution, both to help and learn in the workshop and to attend an evening school which Webster would superintend. After a few months they would return home to teach others what they had learned.

The school was started and Lord Winchilsea and Lady Palmerston both sent men. But the venture was not a success, neither through Webster's fault, nor Rumford's: the anti-Jacobin feeling, in revulsion at the French Terror, was growing stronger; to educate the artisan was not considered safe. Even Mr Wilberforce, who had been enthusiastic to found the RI for the benefit of the working man, supported Pitt's Combination Act of 1800 which forbade workmen's meetings and rallies. Writing years later Webster sadly explained, 'I was not unacquainted with the political feeling of the time but I did not think a little learning was a dangerous thing if *judiciously bestowed*. My idea was to make *good mechanics*, not to force them like hot bed plants out of the sphere in which they are so useful.' In 1802 the school was quietly disbanded. The troubles of the times that had encouraged the founding of the RI also halted its development in this direction. This was a general pattern: enlightened reform as well as radicalism were both slowed almost to a standstill in England by the example of France. Only so much should be done for the workers as would help them to work better and keep their place.

Dr Garnett was duly appointed to be the first Professor at the RI. He was to lecture and to supervise investigations; the result would be published in a Journal of Proceedings. A printing press was bought and a Mr Savage engaged to print and publish the Journals. A journal and a good library were essential to the dignity of a Literary and Philosophical Society; the RI must have an excellent library, and so a Library Committee was appointed. It remained an almost autonomous body until the mid-19th century. Everything at the Institution was to be of the best, the tea and coffee served were top quality, the notepaper supplied in the Conversation Room was gilt edged. No expense was spared; indeed, as Rumford wrote to his daughter in America in March 1801, 'It is a very expensive establishment and will cost a great deal of money – the RI is not only the fashion but the rage – [and it is] gratifying to me to see the honourable list of Lords, Dukes, etc. as fifty-guinea subscribers.'

However, until the Lecture Theatre was ready the Dukes and Lords and their ladies had to crowd for lectures into the room which is now the Library, the audience being accommodated 'with a greater deference to their curiosity than to their convenience'. 'During the winter months the lecture room was crowded with persons of the first distinction and fashion', runs another report; and to avoid traffic blocks in Albemarle Street, coachmen were directed to 'set down and take up' with their horses' heads towards Grafton Street.

Clubs were male, and the few specialised societies existing at that time (soon there would be many more) were almost exclusively male; but the pleasant social atmosphere at the RI has depended to a large extent on the presence and grace of the ladies. They might accompany their menfolk, but from the beginning they were also allowed to join as subscribers in their own right, if considered eligible. In 1800 a committee of seven distinguished ladies, including the Duchess of Devonshire, Lady Bessborough and Lady Palmerston, was appointed to consider and approve those applying.

It was arranged that there should be three lectures a week for serious students of science and that they should be given on Mondays, Wednesdays and Fridays in the evenings at 8 p.m. so that tradesmen and artisans could have the chance of attending after their day's work. At 2 p.m. on Tuesdays and Thursdays there should be general lectures, popular and amusing to attract Fashion and please the ladies. Dr Garnett, the new Professor, would give all the lectures himself. It was a lot to take on, and Garnett had to live and work under Rumford's eye. The lecture terms were to coincide with parliamentary sessions when Society would be in town, January to June.

Thus far Rumford had carried all before him; he had driven, charmed, bullied to get his way. At his best you could describe him as a benevolent despot, but there was something about him that made people uneasy after a while, however intrigued they had been by him at first. There are some little sidelights on his character in Lady Holland's Journal. Before she married Lord Holland she met Rumford in Bavaria when he was working indefatigably for the Elector. 'He was very civil [she writes] and showed me with a degree of minuteness with which I could have dispensed all his hospitals, manufactures, etc.' He clearly fatigued her. In Milan she noted, 'Sir Benjamin dined with me. After dinner, instead of the custom of the country to take a siesta, I took a long-winded discourse . . . upon politics, happiness, mortality etc.' He was an exhausting talker obviously and not a listener, but she could also say, 'Whatever his failings, he is a useful member of society'. There is one other significant comment she makes. She by this time is Lady Holland and he is Count Rumford, and is visiting her house. He 'was entertaining – His manner is soft and plausible, it rather excites distrust and perhaps more than his intentions merit, but there is something suspicious in a kept-down manner.'

Perhaps some of the Proprietors felt the same as Lady Holland, while others were still dazzled, but the Managers became increasingly critical. Mercifully Bernard was there; the patience and steadiness of Bernard had to try and make up for the mercurial behaviour of Rumford. For one thing, Rumford was away so much. He was absent for three periods between the autumn of 1798 and the spring of 1802, in fact for nearly one third of the time. When he was at the Institution the place was a complex of furious activity; when away there was always trouble and delay, and always shortness of cash.

In 1801 Garnett resigned after a rupture with Rumford. He had printed the syllabus of his new course of lectures without reference to Rumford or the Managers; he was worn out too, with his heavy lecture load, and disheartened at not being allowed to being his children to live with him at the RI. He had become listless and melancholy. He died a year later.

Webster left also, early in 1802, disappointed and disheartened by the disbanding of his school. It would not have happened, he felt, if Rumford had not absented himself; he wrote a despairing letter to him in Paris, begging him to return. But in Paris Rumford had other and compelling interests, the *beaux yeux* of Madame Lavoisier, widow of the great French chemist who had perished on the guillotine.

In May 1801 Rumford had made a Progress Report to the Managers which consisted of four lines only about the laboratory and its Professor, the rest being more or less a repeat of his 'Proposals'. In 1802 he made another Report saying that everything was going to plan and swimmingly; yet a week later he suddenly announced that he was arranging for the different departments of the Institution – kitchens, workshops, etc. – to be let out to private contractors and that he was off. He had finished with the RI and its critical Managers. He married Madame Lavoisier in Paris and, alas, lived unhappily with her until they parted. Rumford's Institution was collapsing; but Bernard was there, and the new thread that would lead a very different RI to fame had already been woven in: in 1801 a young assistant lecturer in chemistry had been appointed. His name was Humphry Davy.

TWO

Science and Society

HUMPHRY DAVY

I N THE THREE YEARS since its foundation in 1799 the RI had seen Garnett come and go, Webster come and go, his school for artisans started and disbanded, and now in 1802 Rumford had gone. The Institution was in danger of falling to pieces. Bernard had to come to the fore and he and Coxe Hippisley, Secretary and Treasurer respectively, shouldered responsibility while Mr Savage the printer saw to the daily running of the establishment.

After Garnett's resignation the year before (1801) the Managers had appointed Dr Thomas Young (1773–1829) to be Professor of Natural Philosophy and Superintendent of the House. Young had been recommended to the Managers by Sir Joseph Banks who knew him as scholar, philosopher and Fellow of the Royal Society. Young's name is the first in the long list of RI professors distinguished for their scientific discoveries.

But Young was first a physician. Garnett also was a physician: at that time science and medicine were closely connected and unless the philosopher had private means one of the best ways of cultivating scientific pursuits was from a secure place in the medical profession (though Priestley had managed to combine science with being a Minister). Young saw the RI professorship as an 'occupation which would fill up agreeably and advantageously such leisure hours as a young practitioner of physic must expect to be left free from professional care'. He did not see the RI as a full-time job; but then Young had a phenomenal capacity for work. Davy also, writing to tell a friend in 1801 that he has been appointed at the Institution, says that he will have opportunity and 'as much power as I could reasonably expect secured to me without the obligation of labouring at a profession'. Science was not a profession; it would be nearly another half century before science began to win professional status in its own right.

Young's chief contributions to scientific discovery were in the subjects of sound and light, and he established the theory of interference. In a letter from the RI Davy asked a friend excitedly, 'Have you yet seen the theory of my colleague Dr Young, on the undulations of an Etheral Medium as the cause of Light? It is not likely to be a popular hypothesis, after what has been said by Newton concerning it . . .' Indeed Henry Brougham poured invective on Young, indignant that he should contradict Newton and his corpuscular theory. But Young (as Davy says) 'attempts to revive the doctrine of Huygens and Euler . . . His proofs (i.e. his presumptive proofs) are drawn from some strong and curious analogies which he has discovered between light and sound.'

Young's theory of light gave him the reputation of being the greatest natural philosopher of his day; added to this he was an almost perfect example of the 18th-century ideal of the cultured gentleman with comprehensive knowledge, for he seems to have studied almost all branches, achieving what others only aimed at. He knew Latin and Greek of course (he translated Shakespeare into Greek iambics), had covered all the sciences and mathematics, and spoke most European languages. Sir Henry Holland who was President of the RI from 1865–73 gives a nice description of Young (in his *Recollections of Past Life*):

His profound and various knowledge was concealed under a certain spruce-ness of dress, demeanour and voice which strangely contradicted his Quaker origin, and perplexed those who had known him only from his scientific fame. I have seen the discoverer of some of the grandest and most occult laws of light loitering with ladies in a fashionable shop in Bond Street helping them in the choice of ribbons and other millinery. But what might hastily be deemed affectation was in Dr Young not really such, but genuine courtesy and kind-ness of heart.

Truly a man of very attractive parts.

But Young was not a great success at the RI; he was too independent, too keen to pursue his own researches, and he had little interest in the practical application of science. Indeed, in his introductory lecture, Young hauled up the flag of pure research at the Institution for the first time, declaring that 'the pure spirit of scientific investigation brings its own reward apart from applicable gain'. The RI was not ready for him. Nor was Young a good lecturer: his subjects were too advanced, he was not interested in demonstrations, nor did he seek to entertain his audience. And he did not fit in with the 'useful' objectives of the

Count Rumford, after Kellerhofen

The exterior of the RI in about 1840, by T. H. Shepherd

Sir Joseph Banks by T. Phillips (see p. 39)   Thomas Young, after T. Lawrence

Gillray's cartoon of a lecture, 1802. Rumford is standing by the door on the right, Davy holds the bellows and either Young or Garnett is holding Hippesley's nose

Scientific Researches! — New Discoveries in PNEUMATICKS! — or — an Experimental Lecture o Powers of Air

Institution. In 1803 he resigned to concentrate on his practice as a physician; but he also took up the study of Egyptian hieroglyphs and before he died had deciphered the Rosetta stone.

The next great name in RI history is of course Humphry Davy; he had come to the RI in 1801, marked out for stardom. I must recount something of this fascinating young man's early history. Born in 1778 in Cornwall of an old-established family, Humphry emerged from boyhood with a knowledge of classics, a love of books and a passionate devotion to his native countryside, its sports and the people who lived in it. He loved story-telling and to hold a circle of friends with his tales; it was not so difficult later on to change from raconteur to lecturer. At the age of seventeen he made a list of all the subjects he meant to study for a 'complete' education: all the sciences and history, theology, six languages, mathematics, rhetoric and logic. We do not know how far he got with his programme, but chemistry captivated him. He was apprenticed to an apothecary, heading for a medical career. Chemistry was basic to a physician's training and Davy enjoyed experimenting; almost his first chemical experiments were to disprove a medical theory. In 1772 Priestley had discovered nitrous oxide. It was much discussed and greatly feared, for it was thought to be a carrier of disease. Davy exposed animals to the gas diluted with air and boldly breathed it himself without harmful consequence, indeed he found it exhilarating. He wrote to a Dr Beddoes at Bristol who ran a 'Pneumatic Institution' there where patients came to be treated for various conditions with therapeutic gases, and Beddoes offered Davy a job as his assistant. Beddoes was looked on as rather a quack by the medical profession, but at his Institution Davy had the chance of experimenting further, his allotted task being to research on the curative powers of 'factitious airs'. He dosed himself and his friends with nitrous oxide, the 'pleasure-giving air', and published an account of his work. In it he pointed to the possible use of the pure gas in surgical operations. Had notice been taken of this, anaesthesia might have come in decades before it actually did.

Thus Davy turned away from medicine towards chemistry. It was an exciting time for chemistry, for Lavoisier and the French chemists had been revolutionising it and turning it into a more exact science. In his *Elements of Chemical Philosophy*, published in 1812, Davy wrote of Lavoisier: 'He reasoned with extraordinary correctness upon the labour of others. He introduced weight and measure and strict accuracy of manipulation into all chemical processes.' But Davy could not altogether agree with Lavoisier. In his first scientific papers written in Bristol Davy argued that the first duty of chemists was to show which were simple substances and which were compound. Lavoisier in his *Traité élémentaire de chimie* listed what he considered to be the simple substances, putting Light first, and Caloric (the substance of heat) in second place in his list. Davy challenged the inclusion of heat saying it was not a substance but a motion. Yet he retained light as a substance entering into chemical reactions: it was to be seen in combustion. Davy pushed on with experiments to try and distinguish the compound from the simple substances, but was reaching frustration with the means at the chemist's disposal when a whole new possibility dawned: the agent of electricity, fascinating and mysterious, a phenomenon long known and as yet little understood.

The scientifically minded gentlemen of the 18th century could turn the handle of an electrical machine to make sparks to amuse the company or rub a smooth rod with a rabbit skin to electrify it, as 20th-century schoolchildren do in their first year's physics lessons. Then in 1780 Galvani noticed that a frog's leg twitched when connected with two different metals in an electrical circuit; this caused great excitement and the new reaction was christened 'Galvanism'. The next advance came when Volta found that a solution of copper sulphate would do instead of a frog's leg, and he sent a momentous letter to Sir Joseph Banks in March 1800 announcing his discovery of the 'galvanic pile', the forerunner of our modern electric battery. Men of science rushed to experiment with the pile. Davy with brilliant intuition carefully selected the most hopeful lines to work on, and before the end of the year had elucidated many aspects of galvanic action and published no less than five papers on it. This placed him first in the field and led to his invitation to join the staff at the RI. Davy saw how galvanic action by decomposing the compound substances could lead to the isolation of simple substances and solve the problems of Lavoisier's table; and the RI offered him a laboratory in which to carry out his experiments (but ironically kept him too busy for the next few years to pursue them).

By coming to the Institution Davy abandoned medicine for the time being. But he may have kept open mind about the possibility of returning to it, for as late as 1804 he entered himself at Jesus College Cambridge, presumably with the idea of completing his medical studies. However, success at the R I prevented him doing so. In 1800 it offered dazzling prospects, and not only for chemistry. Society in Bristol had been lively, but at the Institution he would see the great London World of Fashion, listen to and talk with the best intellects of the day: and he would lecture to them. It would be marvellous to hold an audience at the Institution as he had held a band of friends with his tales in Cornwall.

In the spring of 1801 Davy gave his first lecture on 'The New Branch of Philosophy; Galvanism'. He had an immediate success: a report in the *Philosphical Magazine* runs: 'Mr Davy, who appears to be very young, acquitted himself admirably, from the sparkling intelligence of his eye, his animated manner, and the *tout ensemble* we have no doubt of his attaining a distinguished eminence.'

This was most hopeful, and it was only a beginning. Soon it was being reported that 'Men of the first rank and talent, the literary and scientific – blue stockings and women of fashion – eagerly crowded into the lecture room.' Davy's eloquence captured the imagination of his hearers. In his introductory lecture to a course on general chemistry in January 1802 he declared that

In considering and hoping that the human species is capable of becoming more enlightened and more happy, we can only expect that the different parts of the great whole of society should be ultimately united together by means of knowledge and the useful arts . . . In this view we do not look to distant ages or amuse ourselves with brilliant or delusive dreams concerning the infinite improvability of man, the annihilation of labour, disease or even death . . . we look for a time that we may reasonably expect, for a Bright Day of which we Already Behold the Dawn.

Here was glorious hope to lift the hearts of idealists among the listeners. 'The study of nature must always be more or less connected with the love of the beautiful and sublime.' Female hearts melted before the young man's flashing eyes and poetic words and one guesses that the aristocratic gentlemen listened with satisfaction when he claimed 'The unequal division of property and labour, the differences of rank and conditions amongst mankind, are the sources of power in civilized life, its moving causes and even its very soul'. The word 'soul' comes in rather often: Davy spoke of chemistry's appeal to the soul.

Davy was anxious to please, of course, but his enthusiasm was completely sincere: we know that he practised lecturing, but he had the instinctive sense of how to charm and hold an audience. He was brilliant, he was handsome, he matched and captured his hour and drew Fashion to the RI which was just what Bernard and the other Managers wanted. Although he had prided himself on his choice of Davy, Rumford must have watched the situation with some chagrin. The artisans were gone, his Repository for models remained scantily furnished and the lecturing side seemed to be winning so handsomely over that of practical benefit to mankind. The very success of Davy, his type of success, may have contributed to Rumford's decision to throw in his hand and depart some months later. Davy meanwhile was made Professor of Chemistry and had his salary doubled to £200 a year.

Among the aristocratic audience at the RI at that lecture in 1802 there sat a poet, Samuel Taylor Coleridge. He had come to listen to his friend Davy, whom he had met at Bristol. Coleridge holds high place in English literature, but he also has a more modest place in the history of science and in this chapter. The contact between Coleridge and Davy illustrates the link between disciplines when men believed in the Unity of Knowledge, and the strong influence one subject had on another when each could understand much of the other man's subject and even criticize and advise. It was Coleridge, a poet, who after his return from Germany in 1799 had introduced the German philosophy into Cambridge and spread the ideas of Kant.

Coleridge, before laudanum seduced him, had an extraordinary influence on the intellectual world. For this reason it is worth tracing the friendship between Davy and the poet–metaphysician. They first met at Bristol at Mrs Beddoes' house; she was a sister of Maria Edgeworth and liked to collect a literary set in her drawing room. When the two men met, they sparked together. Coleridge was irresistible, full of radical enthusiasm, wild plans and poetic fire. He had enthused the self-centred Wordsworth and bowled over his sister Dorothy. Davy already had a name for a brilliant intellect among the Bristol group and, though he would make his reputation as a natural philosopher, was at that time an aspiring poet. Coleridge, for his part, was very willing to be interested in chemistry. Both were men of the new age of Romanticism. Their youth had been spent in the 18th century, but the mood of the century had been changing as it grew old and they grew up. Davy's thinking shows the change. 'In youth he considered reason as all sufficient', his brother wrote of him, 'while in later life he mistrusted it as inadequate and built his faith on instinctive feeling.' Though he was probably instinctive by nature, he was also chiming in with the trend of the day. 18th-century reason and sense were out of fashion, sensibility and romance were in. The new enthusiasms would have been thought unseemly in Dr Johnson's world of satire and irony, but now the robust taste of the 18th century was softened by a new delicacy. If fashionable sensitivity sometimes verged on the ridiculous, still it was an age that stimulated imagination, gave value to instinct, and loved Nature.

Through Coleridge Davy also came to know Wordsworth. Coleridge and Wordsworth had planned the *Lyrical Ballads* together, and the whole new approach to poetry and poetic diction which Wordsworth would later set out in his famous *Preface*. The three men came to have a huge admiration for each other and one can imagine them striding over the hills, feeling themselves to be the Sons of Genius (at least in the making) as in Davy's poem:

> Like yon proud rocks amid the sea of time
> Superior, scorning all the billows' rage,
> The living Sons of Genius stand sublime,
> The immortal children of another age.

It is fame to be remembered in a novel, and Davy and his poetry as well as his chemistry come into Chapter 2 of *Middlemarch*.

'Sir Humphry Davy?' said Mr Brooke, over the soup, in his easy smiling way – 'Well now, Sir Humphry Davy, I dined with him once at Cartrights and Wordsworth was there too – the poet Wordsworth you know . . . [Davy] was a poet too. Or, I may say, Wordsworth was poet one and Davy was poet two.'

Wordsworth was a poet, Coleridge poet and philosopher, but was Davy to be a poet, or physician, or chemist? A son of which kind of Genius? In the Bristol days he hardly knew. They all aspired to Glory, but it was glory for Poetry, Science, and Mankind rather than for themselves, though they would be glad to bathe in its reflected rays. In the friendship of this trio science and poetry were close in touch. A letter from Wordsworth to Davy has survived, asking him if he will proof-read and correct *Lyrical Ballads*. Another letter written a while later is preserved from Coleridge to Davy enquiring about the possibility and cost of setting up a small chemical laboratory at Grasmere where by that time the Wordsworths had gone to live. Coleridge thought it might be a good idea if he and Wordsworth could study chemistry and do experiments.

William had suffered a depression after his hopes for Freedom had been betrayed by the French Terror and had turned to mathematics for a time, as being unemotional and exact: but Coleridge thought that chemistry might be a more human and imaginative study for him. The laboratory never materialised, it was only one of Coleridge's ideas.

Coleridge and Davy had the same leaping imagination: they were both passionately interested in metaphysics. Wordsworth went along with them but, though he was interested in science, he saw it as lacking the humanity and warm appeal of poetry. Davy's early writings include passages which show that he had absorbed much of his friends' bias towards the prime role of poetry. But after the success of Davy's introductory lecture at the R I in January 1802 the influence starts to flow back the other way. With mounting enthusiasm Davy worked out his forecast of the important role that chemical experiments would play both in developing practical benefits for mankind and in stimulating the human imagination. This eloquence so impressed Wordsworth that in 1802 he enlarged his *Preface* to the *Lyrical Ballads* to include the admission that 'if the time should ever come when what is now called Science . . . shall be ready to put on, as it were, a form of flesh and blood, the Poet will lend his divine spirit to aid the transfiguration', and Poet and Scientist could even become partners in the noble enterprise of social progress. Note that there was still general confidence that Truth was one in a God-centred Universe. The philosopher uncovered the workings of the Creator's plan, the poet hymned its glory. In a letter to Thomas Bernard written in 1804 Davy says, 'I am never more delighted than when I am able to deduce any moral or religious conclusions from philosophical truths. Science is valuable for many reasons, but there is nothing which gives it so high and dignified a character as the means which it affords of interpreting the works of nature so as to unfold the wisdom and the glory of the Creator.' Coleridge's big quarrel with science was that he could not abide figures and hated classification such as occupied the botanists. Davy might have accomplished more if he had followed more method himself. Neither had the humility to plod; they believed in inspiration and instinct. Davy declared in his book *Salmonia* that 'Instincts depend upon influences immediately derived from the Deity'; he followed instinct and made brilliant but somewhat spasmodic discovery.

Davy became immersed in the life of the Institution. 'What a pity such a man should degrade his talents to chemistry,' wrote Godwin to Coleridge. But there he was, acclaimed as a lecturer, friend of the Fashionable, a Fellow of the Royal Society by 1803, recipient of their Copley Medal in 1805. When appointed as Assistant Lecturer he had been led to believe that he would be able to go on with his experiments on Galvanism, but there was never time. First he must give his employers their money's worth by carrying out their behests. For many years yet, Science was to serve an apprenticeship at the R I. 'Investigations' were to be made in the 'complete laboratory' of which the R I was so proud, but it was research done to order of the Managers, and from 1807 organised by a special Research Committee. No great creative work is born of a committee, the creative idea is individual (individual instinct Davy would have called it), though the idea may be worked out by a team, as it usually is in these present days. Davy's research was the first great experimental work to be done at the R I, but for his first six years in Albemarle Street he was almost entirely occupied with valuable 'investigations' carried out to order. It was accepted that science should first of all be useful. Davy published a book in 1812, *The Elements of Chemical Philosophy*. On the first page he says: 'The ends of this branch of knowledge are the applications of natural substances to new uses, for increasing the comforts and enjoyments of man', and secondly, 'the demonstration of the order, harmony, and intelligent design of the system of the earth.'

In 1802 the aristocratic Proprietors of the R I were in the position of having a laboratory at their command and a fine young chemist in charge of it. The idea of helping the poor directly having rather failed, the landlords turned to agricultural problems. After all, to improve their estates must also provide more food and improve the lot of their workforce. Many of the big landowners, as I mentioned in the last chapter, had joined together in a society which they called the 'Board of Agriculture and Internal Improvement'. It was not a Government board, but Pitt had been persuaded to give an annual grant of £3000 for studying the state of agriculture in the country, and its improvement. Sir Joseph Banks was a member of the Board, himself an improving landlord with special interest in sheep breeding. Meetings were held in Sackville Street at the house of the President Sir John Sinclair, himself an R I Proprietor.

Study of soil demands analyses. Sackville Street had no laboratory, but was only a few blocks away from Albemarle Street. What more

reasonable than that a request should be made to the R I Managers for
the use of their laboratory? It was readily granted, for the petitioners
were largely the same people as those who had power to grant the
request. Davy undertook a number of analyses; he became an agricultural chemist and was appointed Chemistry Professor to the Board.
He gave a course of lectures on agricultural chemistry at the R I and the
Board came to listen to him declaring:

Agriculture, to which we owe our means of subsistence, is an art intimately
connected with physical science . . . the knowledge of the composition of soils,
of the food of vegetables . . . is essential to the cultivator of the land . . . and his
exertions are profitable and useful to society, in proportion as he is a chemical
professor. Since indeed the truth has become understood . . . the character of
the agriculturalist has become more dignified and more refined . . . he is aware
of his usefulness to man, and he is become, at once, the friend of nature and the
friend of society.

Davy gave further courses during the next ten years and then
published a book, *Elements of Agricultural Chemistry*, which became the
text book to be found in the library of any improving landlord. But some
people found the new improvements rather high-falutin'. Here is the
chatty Mr Brooke again from *Middlemarch*:

'A great mistake, Chettam', interposed Mr Brooke 'going into electrifying
your land, and that kind of thing, and making a parlour of your cow house. It
won't do. I went into science a great deal myself at one time; but I saw it would
not do. It leads to everything; you can let nothing alone.'

Davy became the friend and trusted adviser of the best society, and
was welcomed as honoured guest at the great country houses. He
attended the annual sheep-shearing at Mr Coke's at Holkham in
Norfolk, stayed with the Duke of Bedford at Woburn, with Lord
Sheffield in Sussex. He shot and fished with them, as well as giving them
agricultural advice: fishing was ever a passion with Davy, along with
chemistry and poetry, and Nelson his hero because he fished with one
arm.

Here is Davy's biographer, Dr Paris, describing him at this time:

His life flowed on like a pure stream, under a sky of perpetual sunshine, not a
gust rustled its surface, not a cloud obscured its brightness. In the morning he
was the sage interpreter of Nature's Laws: in the evening, he sparkled in the

galaxy of fashion; and not the least extraordinary point in the character of this great man, was the facility with which he could cast aside the cares of study – Davy, in closing the door of his laboratory opened the temple of pleasure.

But Society was having its effects on him; as early as 1803 Coleridge was writing to a friend:

I rejoice in Davy's progress . . . [But] it were falsehood if I said that I thought his present situation most calculated of all others to foster either his genius, or the clearness and incorruptness of his opinions and moral feelings. I see two serpents at the cradle of his genius, Dissipation with a perpetual increase of acquaintances . . . with that too great facility for attaining admiration which degrades Ambition into Vanity.

Davy refuted such criticism of himself in a letter to their mutual friend Mr Poole in Somerset, writing, 'Be not alarmed, my dear friend, as to the effect of worldly society on my mind . . . My *real*, my *waking* existence is amongst the objects of scientific research; common amusements and enjoyments are necessary to me only as dreams, to interrupt the flow of thoughts too nearly analogous to enlighten and to vivify.'

If some distraction was necessary, Davy seems to have allowed himself rather a lot; it is said that dashing from his laboratory to his social engagements he often had not time to change his shirt and would pull on a clean one over the old. If one blames Davy for courting Society and allowing himself to be captured by it, one must remember the power that Society wielded then.

In his first year at the RI the Managers directed Davy to study, research into and lecture on 'The principles of tanning leather, and on the Art of Dying and Printing different kinds of cloth': very useful investigations. Leather making was about the fourth most important industry in England at the start of the 19th century; think only of the boots and the saddlery required to get people around, even the common bucket was often of leather. The Northampton shoe industry was already flourishing; it had grown up close to the vast Spencer estates. Landowners had plenty of hides, and tanning leather was the kind of cottage industry landowners were anxious to encourage. But tannin got from oak tree bark was in short supply and it was necessary to find some cheaper substitute. It was not an English problem only: Lady Holland records in her Journal a conversation with Rumford, how he 'was very entertaining, he gave an account of some experiments going on in France on ye tanning matter'.

With three months' leave of absence from Albemarle Street, Davy travelled around the country to study the tanning industry; he made experiments, and at last put forward a recommendation. He suggested that the extract of a type of mimosa from India could be used instead of oak bark. He wrote to his friend Davis Gilbert (later PRS) on 26 October 1802:

– I believe I mentioned to you in a former letter that *Terra Japonica* or Extractum Catechu, contained a very high proportion of the tanning principle. My friend Mr Purkiss, an excellent practical tanner, has lately tried some experiments upon it in a large way. It answers very well, and I am now wearing a pair of shoes, the leather of one of which was tanned with oak bark, and that of the other with *Terra Japonica*; and they appear to be equally good. We are in great hopes that the East India Company will consent to the importation of this article. One pound of it goes at least as far as nine pounds of oak bark.

But the EIC were not cooperative; they had a ready market for Terra Japonica in India and Asia. Relations between the Company and the aristocratic RI never prospered.

Another assignment given to Davy was the assembling of a mineral collection for the RI. Mineral collections were fashionable: geology was a popular subject and there was much interest in rocks and fossils, combined with discussion about the age of the earth. It was a pleasant gentlemanly hobby to chip stones, pick up and dig out fossils on a nice day, and arrange one's own private collection. Mineralogy and geology were also important to the commercial interests of the landowners. Davy spent a summer making a collection for the RI; he had always been keen on geology, so probably had an agreeable time. Bernard accompanied him on part of his travels. Davy had a high regard for Bernard and they got on well together.

Davy had told Poole that his 'real and waking existence was amongst scientific research', but it was not until 1806 that he was sufficiently freed from 'investigations' to do any research of his own choosing; up till then all he had been able to manage was to keep up with what others were doing. It was to serious research on galvanism that Davy returned; he had been longing to get back to it ever since he left Bristol. He constructed a Voltaic pile of enormous size with many cells in series which gave him increased voltage. With it he established the principles of electrolysis and showed that, contrary to what was then believed, only hydrogen and oxygen are evolved when the current flows between the poles in pure (or slightly acidulated) water. He then showed that, when the current is flowing in solutions, alkalis and metals are transferred to the negative poles, and oxygen and acids to the positive poles. This enabled him to foresee the relationship between electrical energy and chemical affinity and the useful part that electric currents could play both in producing chemicals in large quantities for industry and in the discovery of new elements. Davy's discovery opened the way into a new science of electro-chemistry.

Davy sent a paper to the Royal Society which caused a sensation; and, although England and France were at war, Napoleon awarded him his prize for the best 'Galvanic' experiment of the year 1806. Davy's paper was made the subject of the Royal Society Bakerian Lecture for that year. The lecture takes its name from Mr Baker who bequeathed £100 to the RS and died in 1774. The first Bakerian lecture was given by Peter Wolfe, the last of the alchemists, of whom Davy said 'in seeking for brilliant impossibilities they sometimes discovered useful realities' (Davy's *Elements of Chemical Philosophy*). The Bakerian lecture is the great lecture of the year at the Royal and Davy was to give it ten times.

In the following year Davy succeeded in decomposing by his electrolytic method the 'fixed alkalies' soda and potash, and isolated two new elements, Sodium and Potassium. Davy described his experiment, writing soberly, 'There was a liberation of small globules having a high metallic lustre, some of which burst with explosion and bright flame.' But his cousin, Edmund Davy, who was acting as his assistant, relates how when Davy saw this happen he actually danced with joy round the room and it was some time before he was sufficiently composed to continue his experiments.

Davy's fame was prodigious, but overwork in these two years of feverish research brought on a collapse. He was desperately ill for several months and so many enquiries for his welfare were made that health bulletins were posted in the hall of the Institution. The inevitable cancellation of his lectures almost brought the RI itself to collapse for the second time (it was never financially secure for its first fifty years). With no lectures by Davy to offer, subscriptions dropped, and the Institution was dependent on lecture subscriptions for its daily running. The Proprietors had had to provide extra cash to avoid crises before this time; now it was realised that something major must be done. To understand this we must look back a few years.

Since Rumford's departure, the Treasurer Sir Thomas Bernard had been the prime influence in steering the RI into new channels of usefulness, with the Secretary, Sir John Coxe Hippisley to back him in his object of attracting Society. By 1804 the transformation of Rumford's Institution was almost complete. On 6 June 1804 Sir Joseph Banks wrote to Rumford who was leading an uneasy life in Paris with his new wife. Banks had not shared the Managers' criticisms of Rumford.

The Institution has irrevocably fallen into the hands of the enemy, and is now perverted to a hundred uses for which you and I never intended it. I could have successfully resisted their innovations had you been here, but, alone, unsupported, and this year confined to my house for three months by disease [gout] my spirit was too much broken to admit of my engaging singly with the host of H's and B's who had taken possession of the fortress. Adieu then, Institution, I have long declared my intention of attending no more.

So Banks had gone too, but his was the last in the succession of disillusioned departures.

The club interest was strong, the scientific aspect growing, and to the outside world the RI appeared very successful. The Institution provided a stimulating interest in a gloomy time of war, when the Continent was closed and Society could not travel for distraction. Apart from Davy's courses, a wide variety of other lectures was offered, on poetry, the arts, belles lettres. The Reverend Sydney Smith, that kindly wit, filled the lecture theatre to overflowing when he spoke on Moral Philosophy in 1804. A lady wrote a poem 'On buying a new bonnet to go to one of Mr Sydney Smith's lectures'; here is one verse on his audience in the theatre.

> Lo where the gaily vestured throng,
> Fair learning's train, are seen
> Wedged in close ranks her walls along
> And up her benches green.

Rumford in his description of the theatre wrote 'the floors and seats were painted a dark green colour, the seats covered with green moreen cushions.'

Even in Bath ladies gossiped about the RI. Sydney Smith wrote from there to Lady Holland: 'A dreadful controversy has broken out in Bath whether tea is most effectually sweetened by lump or pounded sugar; the worst passions of the human mind are called into action by the pulverists and the lumpists. I have been pressed by ladies on both sides to speak in favour of their respective theories at the RI, which I have promised to do.' Such fashionable gossip was splendid publicity for the RI. Carriages also blocked Albemarle Street when Coleridge lectured at the Institution in 1807. But Coleridge's morale was already beginning to crumble under the 19th-century curse of laudanum addiction. Davy sent this account of him to their mutual friend Poole in Somerset:

... Coleridge, after disappointing his audience twice from illness, is announced to lecture again this week. He has suffered greatly from excessive sensibility, the disease of genius. His mind is a wilderness – with the most exalted genius – he will be the victim of want of order, precision and regularity ... I cannot think of him without experiencing the mingled feeling of admiration regard and pity.

Coleridge wrote to the Managers, 'If I could quit my bedroom I would have hazarded anything rather than not have come . . .' He was let off the rest of his course.

But the financial trouble behind the façade of success at the Institution was acute by 1809. The RI was a private body, the property of its Proprietors; if it were to survive it could remain so no longer. The money the Proprietors had initially put down was insufficient as capital; their rights for tickets curtailed the number of subscribers that could be accommodated, however tightly they crowded the theatre's green benches; and the Institution depended on subscriptions to lecture courses.

For the second time the RI underwent major change, this time to its Constitution. In 1810, by an Act of Parliament and a new Charter, the Proprietors gave up their hereditary rights and were either compensated or made Life Members. Most important of all, the governing body was to be elected no longer by an inner ring, but by the whole body of Members. Thus a wider base was achieved and the RI became a more public organization. Science in the laboratory was still to be 'useful'. But now the Managers threw open their laboratory for public use, and letters were sent to various government departments offering to carry out analyses for them. The RI laboratory was thus the first laboratory to be opened to public use; before this all laboratories had been private.

Previously, investigations had been largely on behalf of the land-owning interest and the RI kept contact with the Board of Agriculture. Indeed Davy, in his lecture on 'The Plan which is proposed for Improving the RI' made a special point of reassuring the landed proprietors that 'whatever specimens they sent for analysis would be carefully examined; their interests would be specially looked after.'

Under the new Charter the RI still maintained its traditional role as the most elegant social and philosophic club in London in spite of retrenchments (the note paper provided no longer had gilt edges and less expensive tea and coffee were served). Membership continued to be sought after for the social enhancement it might bring, and successful merchants and bankers aspired to belong to the RI and rub shoulders with Lords and Earls. Some Indian nabobs joined in the first years, but they were not welcomed by the élite. After 1819 the bankers and nabobs would have the chance to join an Institution more especially designed for them, the London Institution. Founded in 1805 by Sir Francis Baring, a banker and a director of the East India Company, it was closely modelled on the RI, with library, conversation room, laboratory and lecture room, but with an emphasis on commerce and science in its lecture lists. There was courteous exchange between the two Institutions at the LI's founding; Davy was enthusiastic and a number of RI Proprietors joined the LI. In subsequent years RI professors often lectured there. Situated in Finsbury Circus, it was convenient for city merchants and their families who were beginning to people the new suburbs.

Such was the reputation of the RI for scientific solution of technical problems and also as an elegant meeting ground that a number of Institutions sprang up in other centres in emulation: the Cork Society which acknowledged itself to be modelled on the RI, the Surrey Institution, the Royal Institution of Cornwall, the Royal Manchester Institution, and the Liverpool Royal Institution were all founded in the first quarter of the 19th century. It was all very gratifying to the Managers in Albemarle Street. The RI has outlived most of them, the London Institution, its closest parallel, coming to an end in 1912.

Recognition of the worth of Davy's scientific investigations spread in-to other spheres beside that of agriculture. In 1811 he was asked to advise on the ventilation of the old House of Lords. Nothing successful came of this which must have distressed him, especially as it was the Lords, but that same year he had a triumph in Dublin. He was to lecture there and he wrote to his mother, of whom he was very fond: 'The 550 tickets issued for the course by the Dublin Society, at 2 guineas each, were all disposed of the first week; and I am told now that from 10 to 20 guineas are now offered for a ticket. This is merely for your eye; it may please you to know that your son is not unpopular or useless.'

The next year, 1812, saw him honoured, and his life changed. On 8 April Professor Davy was knighted by the Prince Regent; three days later he married; and in between those dates delivered the last lecture of the last course he ever gave at the RI, the course that Michael Faraday listened to from the gallery. They were historic days.

Davy's bride was a wealthy widow, a Mrs Apreece, who had made her salon in Edinburgh, and had ambitions to shine in London intellectual society. He wrote to his mother, 'I shall have great pleasure in making you acquainted with Lady Davy, she is a noble creature . . . and every day adds to my contentment by her powers of understanding and her amiable and delightful tones of feeling.' To enjoy a rich social life with her Davy resigned his professorship at the Institution, but he kept connection with the laboratory, and the next year was appointed Honorary Professor, without salary or obligation to give courses of lectures.

Sir Humphry and Lady Davy planned an extended tour of the Continent the following year, the object of the journey being to study the extinct volcanoes of the Auvergne before proceeding to Italy to examine Vesuvius. It was a tribute to Davy's high reputation that Napoleon, with whom we were still at war, should have granted him permission to enter France; but then Napoleon had already given him a prize. So on 13 October 1813 the Davys left London for Plymouth where they embarked in a 'cartel' bound for Morlaix in Britanny. With them they took Lady Davy's maid, their own carriage (wheels removed for the crossing) a travelling laboratory, and the new young laboratory assistant from the RI who would act as amanuensis and secretary (and do a bit of valeting), whose name was Michael Faraday.

After chafing at Morlaix for a week while their passports were checked, the party at last proceeded to Paris. There the French savants were waiting, anxious to greet 'le Chevalier Davy', and he met Ampère, Gay-Lussac, Cuvier and Humboldt. Sir Humphry and Lady Davy dined with Count Rumford (poor Rumford, broken and tired, had separated from his wife; he died nine months later). The Davys saw the sights, but made a very poor impression themselves. Davy seems to have made no attempt at courtesy in dress or manner; worst of all, he all but trumped his scientific rival, Gay-Lussac, on his home ground. For years they had competed in similar lines of work: when Davy made a qualitative discovery as in the decomposition of the 'Fixed Alkalis', Gay-Lussac quantified it. The former was a romantic discoverer, the latter ordered and related new advance, and between them they served chemistry well. At the time Davy arrived in Paris a *Mémoire* was under review at the National Institute on a strange new substance (noticed by a salt-petre manufacturer) which gave off a purple vapour when heated. Gay-Lussac swiftly investigated and announced his discovery of what he thought to be a new element which he proposed to call 'iode'; Davy experimented with his travelling laboratory and the help of Michael Faraday, and pronounced the strange substance to be a new element, 'iodine'. The two men made their claims almost within hours of each other. Davy characteristically went off to Italy and on to new research, while Gay-Lussac worked out the properties and wrote a long treatise on iode, as it continued to be called in France.

But the rivalry with Gay-Lussac was only one of the influences on Davy's behaviour in Paris; there was also envy on Davy's part for the respected position of science in France under Napoleon's patronage (it was for closer links with the English Government that Davy would press later on as President of the Royal Society). And in the background to all this was national conflict. This visit to Paris, the meeting of intellects across the frontiers of war was an adventurous, unique opportunity; it is sad that Davy should have so mismanaged things as to leave behind him an atmosphere of admiration tarnished with offended disappointment. Scientific rivalry did not justify his arrogance of manner. But in his London world he had also been disappointing his friends. Was he beginning unconsciously to value showing his power over those whose position he envied? Hereditary rank was valuable in those days. It made for stability – but for Davy, heart-burning. Scientific success was not quite enough for him; honours helped. In theory he despised them, but he wrote honestly in his Journal, 'It is not that honours are worth having, but it is painful not to have them'. However, Davy had a generous heart, and on that journey he was kind to young hero-worshipping Faraday for whom Lady Davy had nothing but class contempt.

The Staircase (pre 1798)

Thomas Bernard,
after J. Opie

William Brande,
after L. Wyon

Sir Humphry Davy

From Paris they all proceeded to Montpellier; they crossed the Alps (in mid-winter) into Italy. At Florence Davy burnt a diamond at the Academia di Cimento, using the great burning glass of the Grand Duke of Tuscany. Not that diamonds had not been burnt before. The value of Davy's experiment was in the proof 'that the diamond affords no other substance by its burning than pure carbonic acid gas' – that a diamond, in fact, is composed of pure carbon.

On to Rome, where a large aristocratic and cosmopolitan society was gathered, the Continent being lately re-opened for travel after the Peace of Paris. But plans for much further travel were cancelled by the startling news of Napoleon's escape from Elba. The Davy party turned for home, and after a confusing and difficult journey reached London on 23 April 1815, none of them so glad to be back as Michael Faraday.

When Davy resigned his professorship to go abroad William Thomas Brande had been appointed in his stead. Brande had been lecturing to medical students in Windmill Street, and he transferred his class to the RI, for the next forty years teaching chemistry at 9 a.m. in the basement laboratory which had been made out of the workshop when the artisans disappeared. Brande was rather pedestrian, commercially minded and practical, but he provided a solid continuity of teaching. The Institution must have missed the dash of Davy, as he was missed during his months of illness. Bence Jones records: 'In 1814 during the absence of Sir Humphry Davy the Institution did little for science, but, though poor, it strove to be fashionable. On 23 May it gave a cold collation for the Grand Duchess of Oldenburgh, for which Gunter, of Berkeley Square, was paid by contract twenty guineas.'

Once back in London, Davy returned to work in the laboratory, and immediately became involved in solving a problem which brought him the gratitude of England, indeed of Europe. It was, if you like, a utilitarian problem; the solving of it a supreme example of the usefulness of science. For many years, concern had been growing over disasters in coal mines. The splendid discovery had been made in the 18th century that coal could be used instead of charcoal in blast furnaces and for smelting iron; it was to the extended use of coal that the Industrial Revolution owed so much of its success. More and more coal was wanted, and the new canals transported the coal easily and made it cheap. Mines were dug ever deeper to get out more coal and mine owners got rich, but explosions from fire damp grew ever more frequent, men lost their lives and women mourned.

A terrible explosion had occurred on Tyneside when ninety-two lives were lost, and a Society had been formed in October 1813 to enquire into the disaster. Davy had left for the Continent, but as soon as he got back the Society sought his help. The problem was to design a safe form of light for the miners to carry that would not ignite fire damp, and Davy threw himself head and heart into an investigation. He visited the mines, confirmed that 'fire damp' was the gas methane, studied its explosive power in different proportions of air, and how explosion was conveyed from one vessel to another. Within a few weeks of starting work he had investigated various methods of preventing flame from causing explosions in air containing fire damp, finding that explosions do not pass through small apertures. After several trials he perfected a lamp in which the flame was surrounded by a fine wire gauze, which proved efficient so long as the flame did not heat the gauze. His swift genius had solved a deadly problem. The coal owners presented Davy with a silver dinner service, the Czar of Russia sent him a large silver-gilt vase in recognition of what the 'Davy Lamp' had done for Russian miners, but I think what touched him most was the Tribute of Gratitude from the men at the Whitehaven Colliery with the signatures of the overmen and the marks of seventy-three miners.

Some years later Davy was involved in another national problem. The hulls of H.M. ships of war were covered with copper sheeting to preserve them from destruction by marine borers, but the sheeting corroded in the sea water. The Navy Board asked the Royal Society for advice on how corrosion could be prevented and Davy took on the research himself. His electrolytic experiments pointed a way and he found that when small quantities of zinc or iron were attached to the copper plates they remained uncorroded, proving this with trials in the sea as well as in the laboratory. He wrote a triumphant letter to his brother:

Jan.30th 1824

My dear John

I have lately made a discovery of which you will for many reasons be glad. I have found a complete method of preserving the copper sheeting of ships which readily corrodes. It is by rendering it negatively electrical. My results are of the most beautiful and equivocal kind, a mass of tin renders a surface of copper 200 or 300 times its own size sufficiently electrical to have an action on sea water . . . the saving to the Government and the country will be immense. I am going to apply it immediately to the Navy. I might have made an immense fortune by a patent of this discovery, but I have given it to my country.

Alas, when Davy's protective plates were fixed on actual ships, fouling by weeds and barnacles occurred and the speed of the vessel was so reduced that the scheme was abandoned. Davy was a public figure; there was public criticism, and he was mortified and dreadfully disappointed. He had been so confident. But he had discovered and initiated the principle of cathodic protection.

In 1820 Sir Joseph Banks died and Humphry Davy was elected President of the Royal Society in his place. Banks had dominated the scientific scene for so many years and given the Society a European prominence. He had made a centre at his house, entertaining Fellows and many distinguished foreign men of science to his Thursday breakfasts or his Sunday evening 'Conversations'. Objects of scientific interest were exhibited, and the present yearly 'Conversazione' at the Royal Society derives from Banks's Sunday gatherings. Sir Henry Holland (President of the RI 1865–73) published his *Recollections of Past Life* in 1870. In it he recalls memories of Banks and those meetings he witnessed as a young man:

I was a frequent attendant at the meetings of the Fellows of the Society on Sunday evenings at the house of Sir Joseph Banks in Soho Square [Sir Henry had been elected FRS in 1816]. Amongst those most commonly present were Cavendish, Wollaston, Davy, Young, Chevenix, Davies Gilbert – Dalton also, whom I had well known before in his rude laboratory of broken bottles and other uncouth apparatus at Manchester, appeared occasionally, an individuality himself, apart from the Quaker garb he wore. At these parties . . . the youthful and more elastic genius of Davy came in striking contrast to the inflexibility of Wollaston [who was sternly logical and sceptical] . . . and the hereditary taciturnity of Cavendish . . . [Davy's] early successes in science had emboldened a mind naturally ardent and speculative . . . Sir Joseph Banks himself was necessarily a very conspicuous personage in these parties at his house. Seated and wheeled about in his armchair – his limbs hopelessly knotted with gouty tumours – speaking no other language than English . . . and carrying his scientific knowledge little beyond the domain of Natural History, he nevertheless looked the governing power of the Royal Society, and was such in reality. Sir Joseph Banks, silent in his chair, was more imposing than he would have been if exchanging imperfect phrases, whether of science or courtesy, with the strangers who came to visit him.

This was the figure that Davy succeeded. Banks was hard to follow, and during the seven years of Davy's Presidency a discontent was stirring among the Fellows. No doubt Davy's lack of administrative tact was contributary, but the deep cause was the growing change in the status of science. The Royal Society had been something of a club, for distinguished natural philosophers first, but also for other distinguished people only mildly interested in science: Gibbon, Warren Hastings and Lord Castlereagh had all been Fellows, and Byron was elected in 1816. Banks had linked scientific expertise with the prestige of the aristocracy, as was essential if science was to win a place in the late 18th century, but even before Banks had died, the men of science were beginning to want the Royal Society more exclusively for their own. Davy had too much identified himself with the world of the aristocratic amateur to promote radical reform against the old ways within the Society, but he did try to improve the quality of the Fellowship by sticking more closely to the requirement of scientific attainment in the election of new Fellows, and he had the vision to see that science might play a bigger part in national affairs. His brother John wrote of him, 'It was his wish to see the Royal Society an efficient establishment for the great practical purposes of science . . . having subordinate to it the Royal Observatory at Greenwich for astronomy, and the British Museum for natural history, and a laboratory founded for chemical investigation . . .' Davy hoped that his influence in the great world and his friendship with Sir Robert Peel might be useful in furthering new co-operation, but was unsuccessful in winning support. He foresaw government laboratories, but in this he was before his time. It was not until near the end of the century that the National Physical Laboratory was founded (while in the meantime her state-run laboratories had enabled Germany to get ahead). Davy's idea was another of those conceived in the RI, like Webster's foreshadowing of a technical school, which faded until the time was ripe.

However one very useful project came to fruition: with the help of Sir Stamford Raffles he managed to secure from the Government a grant of land in Regent's Park for the Zoological Society. Davy's effort gave the Zoo its home.

Davy might have done more at the Royal Society if some of his good ideas had been more methodically pursued, but sustained application was not his forte. I think his biographer, Dr Paris, had a shrewd understanding of him. Here is Paris's description of Davy out fishing with Dr Wollaston.

Wollaston evinced the same cautious observation and unwearied vigilance in this pursuit, as so eminently distinguished his chemical labours. The temperament of Davy was far too mercurial: the fish never seized the fly with sufficient avidity to fulfil his expectations, or to support that degree of excitement which was essential to his happiness, and he became either listless or angry, and consequently careless and unsuccessful.

In 1826 Davy's health began to fail and he suffered a stroke which left him partially paralysed. He travelled to Italy on his doctor's advice and then made another journey to the Continent in 1828, travelling slowly with his own horses. In these last years, denied so many of his old occupations, Davy took to writing again. In 1812 he had published his *Elements of Chemical Philosophy* which starts with a brilliant sketch of the history of science from classical times to his own day. In 1813 *Elements of Agricultural Chemistry* appeared and was immediately a best-seller. In 1827 his life-long passion for fishing inspired another little book, *Salmonia*, on an Izaac Walton pattern: four fishermen talk of many things as they go out a-fishing, discuss natural history and the problems of creation. Davy wandered across the Continent for the last time, in 1828, spending the summer in Austria (where in past years he had spent happy times fishing and shooting in the mountains) and proceeding to Italy where he actually did experiments on the electric fish, the torpedo, as he had done with Faraday on the first Continental Journey. There he started writing yet one more book, his last and never finished – the *Consolations of Travel or the Last Days of a Philosopher*. Again this is written in the form of a discussion between friends; they bear classical names and meet in allegorical circumstances. Here Davy the poet is setting forth his scientific speculation, his conviction of an inexhaustible store of knowledge to be explored, and the intellectual delight in its pursuit. His imagination roams freely, but there is a feeling of peace after turmoil, a sense of the Creator, in whom he believed so confidently, upholding all. I quote a passage about his idea of the ideal Philosopher who adventures into new realms.

In announcing even the greatest and most important discoveries the true philosopher will communicate his details with modesty and reserve; he will rather be a useful servant to the public, bringing forth a light from under his cloak when it is needed in darkness, than a charlatan exhibiting fireworks . . . [He] will be humble-minded and a diligent searcher after truth, and neither diverted from the great object by the love of transient glory or temporary popularity . . . He should resemble the modern geometrician in the greatness of his views and the profoundness of his researches, and the ancient alchemist in industry and piety . . . and in contemplating the variety and beauty of the external world, and developing its scientific wonders, he will always refer to that Infinite Wisdom, through whose beneficence he is permitted to enjoy knowledge.

This could be read as a portrait of Michael Faraday, Davy's successor at the RI.

Humphry Davy, 'the greatest chemist of his age', died in Geneva on 1 May 1829.

MICHAEL FARADAY
1791 – 1867

THREE

The Scientific Quest

MICHAEL FARADAY

WHEN Humphry Davy died in 1829 Faraday had long been the leading figure at the RI, having been Superintendent of the House since 1821 (living there with Sarah his wife) and Director of the Laboratory since 1825. In 1829 Michael Faraday FRS was 38, established as the distinguished natural philosopher at the Institution.

So much has been written about Faraday, the most fascinating figure in 19th-century science, but so good a story can bear sketching again. It must be re-told to explain how he altered the very regard for science by his discoveries and stabilised the position of the RI. The Institution was more than fortunate to have two such men as Davy and Faraday in its first half century. Each gave what was needed in his time; Davy lit a fire and under Faraday it glowed.

Each came as a young man, Davy aged 23, Faraday at 21. But they were poles apart in personality and their circumstances utterly different. Davy had aimed at acquiring the gentleman's 'comprehensive education'; Faraday, son of a blacksmith, came to the RI as a bottle-washer with no education save the three Rs and what he had found for himself. Davy spoke to the great with confident charm; young Faraday's voice was probably a little too careful, for he was trying with desperate earnestness to improve himself, his manners and his expression.

Among all the examples of self-taught geniuses, Michael Faraday is unmatched. History seems to show that the genius will reach his height whether he is given education or not; he will find what he needs by himself. The boy Michael, apprenticed to a bookseller, a Mr Riebau, read the books he was given to bind. It was chance that led him into science: he found a copy of the *Encyclopaedia Britannica* and came across the article on electricity; he bound Mrs Marcet's *Conversations on Chemistry* published in 1809 for audiences created by Davy. Enthusiastic to try the experiments she described, he built himself a small voltaic pile. When he needed a furnace, he used the fireplace in Mr Riebau's back room (Riebau was a kind man) and fifty years later wrote, 'When I questioned Mrs Marcet's book by such little experiments as I could find means to perform and found it true to the facts as I could understand them I felt that I had got hold of an anchor in chemical knowledge and clung fast to it.' He saw a notice for some science lectures that a Mr Tatum was giving at his house in Dorset Street, and his brother gave him the shilling for a ticket.

The books in Riebau's shop were Faraday's library and he read voraciously. A school syllabus organizes information, but Faraday was collecting a squirrel hoard of heterogeneous facts when he came across Dr Isaac Watts' *Improvement of the Mind*, and this book provided a clue for someone who did not know where he was going or how to proceed. The book set out a plan for self-education; Faraday decided to follow Dr Watts's advice.

First, he must learn to express himself. He started a long correspondence with an acquaintance he had made at Mr Tatum's house, Benjamin Abbott, for, as he explains in his first letter to Abbott, 'the great Dr Isaac Watts (great in all the methods respecting the attainment of learning) recommends it as a very effectual method of improving the mind of the person who writes and the person who receives.' Faraday describes experiments he has seen performed and lectures he has heard, and observes and moralizes in a somewhat heavy priggish way. Although acquaintance rapidly became friendship and they met frequently, he went on writing and Abbott kept those letters that show Faraday adventuring into a new world. The happy thing is that no strain ever developed with his family which he was intellectually outgrowing; mutual affection and their religious faith kept them together.

Dr Watts suggested ways of collecting and storing information; young Faraday cut out articles from unsold magazines lying around at Riebau's and filed them in scrapbooks. With a group of friends from the City Philosophical Society (the Society that met at Mr Tatum's) he organised a Mutual Improvement Plan to meet and discuss and criticize each other's speech and writing; they were desperately serious. But it was not so all the time. Faraday could make a plan to meet Ben Abbott at Ranelagh for an outing, could be distracted from work by his delight in a band, and could write at the beginning of a very long letter of shrewd comment on lecturing: 'Dear Abbott, As when on some secluded branch . . . sits perched an owl who full of self conceit and self created wisdom, explains, comments, condemns, ordains and orders things not understood, yet full of his importance still holds forth to stocks and stones around – so sits and scribbles Mike . . .' This letter is dated 1813 and was written from the RI. I quote another letter that Faraday wrote sixteen years later in a very different vein, to explain how he got there. The letter is addressed to Dr Paris, Davy's biographer.

Royal Institution, Dec 23 1829

My dear Sir,

You asked me to give you an account of my first introduction to Sir H. Davy . . . When I was a bookseller's apprentice I was very fond of experiment and very adverse to trade. It happened that a gentleman, a member of the RI [Mr Dance] took me to hear some of Sir H. Davy's last lectures in Albemarle Street. I took notes and afterwards wrote them out more fully in a quarto volume.

My desire to escape from trade, which I thought vicious and selfish, and to enter into the service of Science which I imagined made its pursuers amiable and liberal, induced me at last to take the bold and simple step of writing to Sir H. Davy, expressing my wishes and a hope that if an opportunity came in his way he would favour my views; at the same time I sent the notes I had taken of his lectures [The RI preserves the manuscript book, exquisitely set out and written] . . . You will observe that this took place at the end of the year 1812; and early in 1813 he requested to see me . . . [Bence Jones records how Davy's carriage drew up at the door one evening just as Faraday was undressing to go to bed, and a letter was delivered inviting him to call at the Institution the next morning; and when Faraday presented himself Davy] told me of the situation of assistant in the laboratory of the Royal Institution, then just vacant.

At the same time that he thus gratified my desires as to scientific employ-ment, he still advised me not to give up the prospects I had before me, telling me that Science was a harsh mistress . . . He smiled at my notion of the superior moral feelings of philosophic men, and said he would leave me to the experience of a few years to set me right on that matter.

Finally, through his good efforts, I went to the Royal Institution early in March 1813, as assistant in the laboratory [at 25 shillings a week with two rooms in the attic and candles] and in October of the same year went with him abroad as his assistant in experiments and in writing.

The continental journey with Davy served Faraday as his Grand Tour. He had been seven months at the RI when they set off; he had been working and reading the library books, watching and commenting to Abbott on experiments, on lectures and lecturers, but as yet he knew nothing of the aristocratic social world of the RI Members. He was to learn a lot on the journey, about people as well as about chemistry.

Faraday kept a journal for those two years of travel. It is fascinating to read the impact of strangeness on his fresh brilliance, his innocence and inexperience, but I can only quote a few scraps. I have already told something of Davy on the journey, but here are some of Faraday's impressions along the same route.

He saw great sights in the two years away, but I think that the most exciting moment of all was at the very beginning, on the way to Plymouth. 'I was more taken by the scenery today than by anything else I have ever seen. It came upon me unexpectedly, and caused a kind of revolution in my ideas respecting the nature of the earth's surface.' The scenery was 'the mountains of Devonshire', and they startled him more than did the Alps later on, for he had 'acquaintance with no other green surface than that within three miles of London'. Then came first sight of the sea and the crossing by night to Brittany:

I remained on deck and escaped all sea-sickness – and watched the luminous appearance of the sea – [and] as day came on and the light increased we looked about us and saw nothing – except sky and immense waves striding one after another – these as they came to us lifted our small vessel and gave us when on their summits a very extended horizon; but we soon sank down into the valleys between them and had nothing in view but the wall of water around us.

He makes a picture; practice in writing had been beneficial. Arrived in port, he looked on the bustle with the traditional English traveller's contempt for the Froggies as they 'poured on [our packages] and conveyed them in every direction – with such an air of business and importance, and yet so ineffectually'. He comments on the good food and the dirty kitchen at the inn, and on the road to Paris marvels at the postilions leaping straight into their great jack boots lashed to the saddle. In the darkness he sees a GLOW-WORM for the first time and records it in capitals in his Journal. There follows a careful study of glow-worms and many years later he gave a Friday Discourse on them at the RI.

In Paris he wandered rather lonely, 'the only Englishman not in custody' (we were still at war); he saw Napoleon driving in the rain, huddled in an ermine cloak, visited the Galerie Napoléon at the Louvre where he gazed at the Emperor's looted treasures on display, 'amongst them the Apollo, the Laocoon, the Venus de Medices, the Heracles, the Gladiator dying and many more of the finest pieces of the ancient Greek Masters', and makes the comment, 'It is both the glory and the disgrace of France.' He has shrewd things to say about the interiors of French houses:

In the internal decoration of apartments the French apply glass and marble, two beautiful materials . . . in brass working too they have also risen to great perfection; [but, he sums up] French apartments are magnificent, English apartments are comfortable; French apartments are highly ornamented, English apartments are clean; French apartments are to be seen, English apartments enjoyed; and the style of each kind best suits the people of the respective countries.

He was glad he was an Englishman.

Curiosity about creatures and things, and especially things scientific, shrewd observation of men and manners, these went hand in hand with a vaulting imagination; and he was stirred by the romance of travel. They had left Paris and were following the Loire valley before a winter's dawn.

. . . though only assisted by the faintness of starlight I am sure our road was beautiful; 'twas along the banks of the river within a few yards of the water which indeed at times came to our horses' feet . . . 'Tis pleasant to state almost audibly to the mind the novelty of present circumstances – that the Loire is on my right hand, that the houses to the left contain men of another country to myself, that it is French ground I am passing over . . . we seem tied to no spot, confined to no circumstances; at all hours, at all seasons, and in all places we move with freedom – our world seems extending and our existence enlarged; we seem to fly over the globe, rather like satellites to it than part of it, and mentally take possession of every spot we go over.

Italy was the party's destination; a band of sixty-five men hauled the carriage, with wheels removed, and the travelling laboratory and the baggage, on sledges over snow-covered Col de Tende, and carried the humans in *chaises à porteur*, save for Faraday who walked in double set of clothing and nightcap, barometer in hand. Turin, Florence, Rome and Naples; the journey had for him highlights of scientific interest, moments of terrible homesickness, and of indignation at Lady Davy, who treated as a servant the young man who was becoming a natural philosopher in his own right. Everything came under Faraday's sensitive observation, the ways of the world as well as the combustion of diamonds, Vesuvius and the torpedo fish, iodine and glow-worms, carnivals, Napoleon and the rest. Faraday wrote home about it all to Abbott and to his mother, and his last letter to her to tell her that he was about to arrive back ends, 'the sweetest letter I ever wrote you'. He had learned so much, but home was all he wanted.

They were back and the RI was still there. Rumour had reached them in Italy that the Institution was in financial straits; it was still living from hand to mouth, and the absence of Davy abroad meant financial loss, just as when he was ill and unable to lecture for months in 1807–8. Faraday had written to Abbott to save his books if there were a crisis. However Faraday was reinstated in his old job with wages raised to 30 shillings a week. He had left in 1813, temporary valet and scientific amanuensis to Humphry Davy; he returned in 1815, the matured traveller who during the next year delivered six lectures to the City Philosophical Society on the properties of matter. It was only six years since his brother had given him the shilling to go to his first scientific lecture there. He might have been pleased with himself, but he declared, 'I have learned just enough to perceive my ignorance', and he re-started the Mutual Improvement Society.

Faraday's duties at the RI were to help Professor Brande; he prepared demonstrations for Brande's morning lectures to his medical students and later gave some of the lectures himself. Brande may not have fulfilled Faraday's romantic idea of the natural philosopher, and he is not remembered for remarkable research work, but he was providing some of the best science teaching in London, and making a small but steady contribution to the Institution's finances by handing over one third of the fees he received from students.

The RI was then at the height of its utilitarian phase, solving many problems in agriculture and industry by the investigations carried out to order in its laboratory. Faraday was directed to make analyses of sugar beet, and he even appeared as expert witness in a patent suit over sugar refining: the voice of science being so well respected in the 19th century, it was a way scientists could make money. Science expected to be used; through all the first half of the century what scientists could do practically was almost more important than what science was discovering. Faraday himself declared in a lecture in 1816 that the attitude of an experimentalist to a new fact should be: 'Endeavour to make it useful'. The Benthamite ideology of reform pervaded the thinking world and the Utilitarians sought to employ science in the attempt to solve the difficulties caused by an exploding population and urban expansion; water supply, sewage and sanitation were problems that plagued the country for many decades. Science was the new weapon with which to fight for public health. So scientists were consulted, and many samples were sent to the RI for analysis. Faraday became an expert water analyst, as Frankland, Dewar and Crookes were fifty years later. In 1857 the National Association for the Promotion of Social Science was founded and, in the effort to study problems scientifically, lists of facts and figures were collected and studied as never before, and vital statistics became a recognised science. The end was laudable, but perhaps the means to it interested the Utilitarians over much. Sydney Smith had never liked them. 'That school treat mankind as though they were machines, the feeling and affections never enter into their calculations.'

Maurice Berman in his book *Social Change and Scientific Organisation: The Royal Institution 1799–1844* complains that science at the RI (during the earlier part of the 19th century) was the tool of capitalism, and one must agree that it was so anyway for the first decade of its existence, when the entrepreneurial landlords used the scientific expertise of the Institution largely to solve their agricultural problems. But I maintain that the RI was a willing servant rather than a tool during that decade, for after all it was the Proprietors' Institution; they owned it, they payed the piper and called the tune. Davy served them willingly to gain their patronage for science, and was very successful in persuading them that science was worth investing in. In 1810 when the aristocratic landlords had mostly departed after the reorganisation and the RI had become a public body with a laboratory thrown open to outside request, it became the turn of the Utilitarian interest to employ science for the benefit of society as a whole. Given the RI aim to be useful (the work can be thought of as an extension of Rumford's aim of benefiting and increasing the comforts of the poor) and given the RI's dire financial straits, it was natural and necessary that the Institution should engage in 'useful' science investigations for which it received payment. Faraday, come to maturity as a philsopher in such a tradition, was the loyal employee of the Institution, carrying out hundreds of analyses with skilful hands trained in the book-binding trade. He gained a reputation as a chemist and an expanding practice as a scientific consultant.

The two biggest projects that Faraday carried out to order were investigations into alloys of steel, and into optical glass. He started experimenting on steel in 1818 and the work continued over the next five or six years. He visited steel works in South Wales and enjoyed the clanging and banging and the sparks which reminded him of his father's smithy. He made numerous alloys, and was rather fond of giving presents of razors made of his best steels to his friends.

The other even longer task was some research to improve the manufacture of optical glass, begun in 1825 at the request of the astronomer Herschel and the Royal Society. Faraday had a furnace built in the RI basement, and an ex-sergeant of the Royal Artillery called Anderson was engaged to stoke for him. Anderson became his devoted assistant for forty years, loyal and so unquestioning that once, it is recorded, Anderson went on stoking the furnace all night because Faraday forgot to tell him to stop and go to bed. He was the only assistant Faraday ever had, but then Faraday liked it that way; he would base no theory on an experiment he had not carried out himself.

But before I attempt any description of Faraday's scientific achievement, I must try and tell of what was fundamental to him, his religion. I believe that it was his religion which gave him that vision of the Universe that guided his research and gave him the strength of conviction with which he pursued scientific truth.

The Faraday family belonged to a small fundamentalist sect called Sandemanians. They believed most earnestly in Salvation, that Christ has saved his followers by the Cross, and they held that man can never be thankful enough and that his whole life should be directed to showing his gratitude. They were a close knit community, they looked after each other and found satisfaction in their own group, heeding and friendly towards, but not needing, the rest of the world. Serene, with confidence in their Salvation, they lived somewhat secluded.

Living in awe and thankfulness to your God and looking after your neighbour is a fine conception of life and a great ideal. Faraday lived for it and by it and spent his days uncovering the laws of the Universe his God had made. But he claimed absolute distinction between scientific and religious belief, confident that each held a different aspect of Truth. They were as parallel lines, and one guesses that Faraday was content to let them meet in Infinity. Some theologists and some scientists have tried to reconcile them too soon.

A Sandemanian generally married another and that is what Faraday did. With charming hesitancy he courted Miss Sarah Barnard, and they married in 1821. They remained all in all to each other for the rest of their days. Faraday was permitted to bring his bride to live at the R I and was given two more rooms. It was a happy cheerful home; alas they had no children, but family and young people were in and out, and for years a favourite niece lived with them. She has told how her uncle helped her with her lessons and when she visited him in the laboratory he would drop a piece of potassium in a bowl of water for her to watch it spin; sometimes she and her aunt went down and installed themselves in a corner of the laboratory when he was working late. There were children's parties when a velocipede was ridden in the corridor round the back of the theatre, so it is said.

The Faradays had no social ambition; Sarah Faraday must have been the perfect wife for a scientist, understanding his need to go broody on research and let the rest of life go a bit out of focus at times. Her husband needed much quiet. From early days he suffered from headaches, and as the years went on he was forced to seek relief from the excitement and tension of his work. They would go for a few days to Brighton or the Isle of Wight, and once for three months to Switzerland where he went for enormously long walks, up to twenty or thirty miles.

If Faraday had only concerned himself with chemistry he would be remembered as a great chemist, but the discoveries for which he is the more famous are electrical. For these he would now be called a physicist.

It was hero-worship of Davy that inspired Faraday's interest in chemistry, and working with Davy that made him a chemist. In those years after they returned from the Continental journey, as well as doing countless analyses and assisting Brande, Faraday helped Davy in his researches. One day in March 1823 Faraday had been working with Davy on an investigation into a gas, chlorine hydrate. That same evening Dr Paris (Davy's biographer) was to dine with the Davys, but, arriving early, slipped down to the laboratory to see if Faraday was there, and found him engaged on an experiment with the gas under pressure in a sealed tube.

It appeared to me that the tube in which he was operating upon the substance contained some oily matter and I rallied him upon the carelessness of employing soiled vessels. Mr Faraday, upon inspecting the tube acknowledged the justness of my remark – in consequence of which he immediately proceeded to file off the sealed end; when to our great astonishment, the contents suddenly exploded and the oily matter vanished.

Dr Paris could not wait while Faraday repeated the experiment, but told Davy the story at dinner. Davy looked thoughtful. Next day Paris received the following note: 'Dear Sir, The *oil* you noticed yesterday turns out to be liquid chlorine. Yrs faithfully Michael Faraday.' Chlorine had been liquefied for the first time. Faraday succeeded in liquefying several other gases, but the more difficult ones had to wait till the end of the century for James Dewar and his more sophisticated methods, and the great machine which Dewar built in the RI basement.

Another discovery of the period once again came from noticing a residue in a container, this time a gas cylinder. Faraday's brother was engaged in the business of house-to-house delivery of cylinders of coal gas under pressure, for illumination. After the gas had been used, a little fluid was always left in the cylinder; Faraday analysed it and isolated a new substance which he called bicarburet of hydrogen, but is now called benzene. It was a productive discovery; benzene is the basis of half organic chemistry, and from it has stemmed the vast dye industry.

Electricity had been the great fascination for Faraday ever since he read the article in the Encyclopedia in Riebau's shop and wrote excitedly to tell Abbott he had built a voltaic pile for himself. He had listened to lectures on electricity and questioned theories, for electricity was the great mystery. Magnetism was another, and it was Faraday who would work out the true relation between electricity and magnetism and become the greatest in the chain of discoverers (beginning with Galvani and Volta) whose names map the laws of electricity, so that volts, and amps and ohms have come into the language, and schoolchildren learnt that Signor Volta divided by Monsieur Ampère equals the resistant Herr Ohm. Later James Watt added his English name to the international series. Later still Faraday's has been used for units of electrical quantity, and units of electrical capacity have been named 'farads'. Through his study of connection between electricity and magnetism Faraday transformed electricity from the philosopher's mystery and the gentleman's toy into a power which would run the world, and by his electrical researches he changed scientific thinking.

What was electricity? This is the question that philosophers were asking in the early 19th century. It was always a temptation to pre-suppose a fluid when actions were not understood. Phlogiston had for long been the supposed agent of burning, caloric of heat, and now electricity could most easily be thought of as a fluid (the potential difference between poles being so like a difference in water pressure in a pipe). There was a one-fluid theory, and Faraday had shown great daring in his youthful days defending a two-fluid theory against the weight of general scientific opinion. And then Faraday abandoned fluid theories altogether.

In 1820, Oersted in Copenhagen had shown that an electric current could deflect a magnetic needle, and one day in 1821 Wollaston and Davy came to the RI to make an experiment with a magnet and a wire. Faraday watched and thought, and experimented further; and on Christmas Day 1821 he triumphed. He succeeded in making his current-carrying wire rotate round a magnet, and he called his wife down from preparing their first Christmas dinner together to watch his spinning wire. He had made a great discovery in electro-magnetism.

He rushed to publish a paper in the *Quarterly Journal*, but then joy began to fade. Faraday's discovery derived from Wollaston's work and Faraday had tried to clear the situation with him before publication, but Wollaston was out of town. Faraday did not like to describe Wollaston's experiment without his consent and the *Journal* went to press with no mention of Wollaston's name in the paper. A sorry rumour began to circulate that the laboratory junior at the RI had trespassed on the great Wollaston's ground. Faraday's triumph and Sarah's pride in her husband turned to dust. Davy was indignant; Wollaston accepted an explanation and the storm settled slowly, but when Faraday's name was put forward for the Royal Society in 1823 it stirred again and Davy asked Faraday to withdraw his candidature. When he was elected in 1824 there was one black ball.

Faraday remained totally loyal to Davy and would never listen to criticism of him; Davy had been kind to him in his anxious early days and had signed himself 'your sincere well wisher'. But it is easier to be generous to a hero-worshipping junior than to a man who is catching you up. At their first meeting Davy had smiled at Faraday's notion of the superior feelings of scientific men. Ten years later Faraday had painful experience of the pitfalls and codes of scientific life, and the law of trespass and priority. Most natural philosophers (except Davy) can do without wealth or social distinction. The prize for them is the honour of discovery; over that your philosopher can be as jealous as anyone else.

Throughout the rest of the 1820s Faraday was too busy to explore further in the subject of electro-magnetism. He had the two big investigations on his hands, into steel and optical glass, and he was moving into a position of responsible prominence at the Institution. Davy came less and less, with the Royal Society Presidency occupying him and his health beginning to decline. In 1824 Faraday began to lecture and his modesty and enthusiastic charm soon won the hearts of his audience. He was Director of the Laboratory, he started the Friday evening Discourses in 1826, and in the same year the famous series of Juvenile Lectures at Christmas time. There was so much to do. Although the scientific world was pondering on the subject of electro-magnetism, it was not until Faraday had relinquished his glass investigations in 1831 that he felt free to seek answers to the questions that must have been seething in his own mind.

Electricity could produce magnetism; could not magnetism be made to produce electricity? Also, just as a magnet could make another temporary magnet out of any piece of iron close to it, should not an electric current in wire produce another current in a wire alongside it?

At last in 1831 Faraday hit upon the truth in two crucial experiments. In August he prepared an iron ring wrapped round with two separate coils of insulated wire (home made, for there was none to be bought) and he found that when he passed a steady current through one coil no effect could be observed in the other, but that when the current was switched on or off in the first coil, a responding current ran through the second. *Only a changing current can induce.* Such is the truth Faraday established that day, thereby laying the basis upon which alternating current transformers have since been developed.

Then in October of the same year in another equally important series of experiments he showed that by moving a permanent magnet through the centre of a coil of insulated wire, an electric current could be created in the wire. This is the basic principle of the dynamo.

Gradually Faraday mastered the principles involved. It became clear to him that it was not within the wires or the magnet that the forces lay, but that the seat of the force was in the space between. He had a large (12 ft.) conducting hollow cube built and mounted so that it could be charged by an electrostatic machine till the sparks flew from its corners while he sat peacefully inside; thus proving that there was no electricity within the charged cube, it was all on the surface.

That the forces are in the space between the charged bodies is true both for electrical and magnetic forces, and Faraday plotted the 'lines of force' as he called them, by scattering iron filings on a sheet of paper lying over a magnet and watching the filings arrange themselves along those lines. This is an easy and charming experiment to repeat, but Faraday must have watched with awe when he first saw this visible map of his invisible forces. He expressed his feelings, writing to his friend Professor Matteucci a quarter of a century later, 'The use of lines of magnetic force . . . as true representations of nature, is to me delightful, and as yet never failing'.

The course of his work can be traced in his *Diary of Experimental Researches*, the day-to-day record of his thoughts, his experimental successes and failures, all neatly numbered. The Diary was printed and published between 1932 and 1936, after the centenary of his famous experiment with his ring.

Another important set of investigations was concerned with the forms of electricity. Were the different forms of electricity – frictional, voltaic and others – the same or no? There had been discussions and doubt about this; Faraday compared their effects and proved that, 'Electricity, whatever may be the source, is identical in its nature'.

Then he proceeded to try and measure electricity, for no means were known. He did it by electrolysis, taking as his measure of electricity the volume of gases contained. Next he proved that the products of electrolysis of a compound were proportional in quantity to their chemical combining weights. This was to take up Davey's qualitative work on electrolysis and determine the quantitative laws of electrochemistry.

A number of new names had to be coined to describe the new phenomena, so Faraday consulted Whewell, the Master of Trinity College, Cambridge. It was proper to have classical roots for the new words, and Faraday had no classics. Anode and cathode, electrode and electrolyte are some of the new words they devised after much correspondence. Whewell did more for science than coin words for Faraday: he coined the very title 'Scientist'. In his *Philosophy of Inductive Sciences* (1840) he defends the creation of new words: 'we may make such words when they are wanted. As he cannot use "physician" for a cultivator of physics, I have called him a *physicist*. We need very much a name to describe a cultivator of science in general. I should incline to call him a *scientist.*' This might do for others, but Michael Faraday preferred to remain a natural philosopher.

In order to concentrate on his electrical investigations in the 1830s, Faraday took on no more analyses; he declined invitations and gradually gave up his outside work as expert witness and scientific consultant which had brought him in a comfortable income (of which he gave away a considerable portion to charity). He had needed to make some money, for the RI could pay him so little; but in 1833 the Institution found a benefactor. Let Professor Gladstone explain:

Up to 1833 Faraday was bringing the forces of nature in subjection to man on a salary of only £100 per annum, with house coal and candles, as the funds of the Institution would not at that time afford more; but among the sedate habitués of the place was a tall jovial gentleman, who lounged to the lectures in his old fashioned blue coat and brass buttons, grey smalls and white stockings, who was a munificent friend in need. This was John Fuller, a Member of Parliament. He founded Professorships of Chemistry and Physiology with endowments that bring in nearly £100 a year each, and gave the first appointment to Faraday for life.

It is said that Fuller appreciated the RI because he could sleep so well in the lectures; others since have also found the lecture theatre soporific.

Through the decade of the thirties the strain of so much concentrated and exciting research work was telling on Faraday's health. Headaches increased; at the RI he was living, so to speak, 'over the shop' and the temptation would be to work long hours and work late. I cannot help feeling myself that the RI basement was a most unhealthy air-less place to work in, though the rides he sometimes took to Hampstead Heath on his velocipede in the early mornings must have helped.

A holiday for several months in Switzerland in 1835 enabled Faraday to carry on, but in 1840 he had a complete breakdown; mind and body were exhausted and his memory was slipping. He had to rest completely for a year, and it was not until 1845 that he returned to steady work in his laboratory. But if they were fallow years, one guesses that much was going on under the fallow; for in 1845 he began another great series of electrical experiments, and this new development of his researching was directly influenced by his philosophic and religious outlook.

In the early 19th century there was a strong belief in underlying Unity. God had made the world, it was a whole, so surely everything in it must be connected. This was the belief of thinking people who were religiously minded, and most people were that. It was not a new idea, the ancients had thought about it. Here is Boethius writing around 500 AD:

> This discord in the pact of things
> This endless war 'twixt truth and truth
> That singly hold, yet give the lie
> To him who seeks to yoke them both,
> Do the gods know the reason why?
>
> Or is truth one without a flaw
> And all things to each other turn,
> But the soul, sunken in desire,
> No longer can the links discern
> In glimmering of her smothered fire?

And here is Davy (in a lecture taken down by young Faraday in 1812): 'When the laws which govern in chemical science are fully known, there is no doubt that it will become a much more simple science . . . It will, I have no doubt, connect mechanical and chemical sciences together; it will concentrate them into one, and in that one comprehend the Universe . . .' Davy went on to express his hopes in poetic rhetoric: 'Let [the philosopher] turn his thoughts to general views . . .' and this is what Faraday did in the 1840s.

He had complete confidence in a world designed by God; in such a world everything must be ordered and connected and Faraday set about uncovering the connections with increasing intensity. There may be conviction of the heart, but the philosopher must not assert his conviction until it has been proved by experiment. Faraday spent the rest of his working life in the search and never lost faith even when he failed to establish links that others found later. But his faith helped him to establish important ones.

He had already connected electricity and magnetism; light, heat and gravity, he thought, must also be connected with them. He searched for a relation between electricity and light, and (after long effort) succeeded in showing that an electromagnet would alter the polarisation of a ray of polarised light passing through a piece of heavy glass he had made in the course of his optical glass investigations. He records triumphantly, 'Thus magnetic force and light were proved to have relation to each other.' Whewell wrote to congratulate him: 'I cannot help believing that it is another stride up the ladder of generalisation, on which you have been climbing so high and standing so firm.'

By his work on electrolysis, following on Davy's, Faraday had already established the relation of electricity to chemical action: but would it be possible to establish a connection between magnetism and gravity? On 19 March 1849, he wrote in his notebook:

'Gravity. Surely this force must be capable of an experimental relation to electricity, magnetism and the other forces, so as to bind it up with them in reciprocal action and equivalent effect. Consider for a moment how to set about touching this matter by facts and trial . . .' But his notebook entry on this subject ends, '*All this is a dream.* Still examine it by a few experiments. Nothing is too wonderful to be true, if it be consistent with the laws of nature; and in such things as these, experiment is the best test of such consistency.' He sent a paper to the Royal Society which finishes thus: 'Here end my trials for the present. The results are negative; they do not shake my strong feeling of an existence of a relation between gravity and electricity, though they give no proof that such a relation exists.'

The relation was not found until Einstein had developed his theory of relativity, and astronomical observations on an eclipse in Brazil had been carefully measured. Then it was proved that a ray from a star had been bent by passing close to the sun: electromagnetic waves were being deflected by the sun's mass. Gravity and electricity *are* linked.

Faraday wrote out his notes for a lecture he was to deliver before Prince Albert in 1848; they begin:

The exertions in physical science of late years have been directed to ascertain not merely the different natural powers, but the manner in which they are linked together . . . and their probable unity in one. [The lecture was on magnetic and diamagnetic bodies, and he ends] . . . and when we remember that the earth itself is a magnet, pervaded in every part by this mighty power, universal and strong as gravity itself, we cannot doubt that it is exerting an appointed essential influence over every particle of matter. . . What its great purpose is seems to be looming in the distance before us. The clouds which obscure our mutual sight are daily thinning, and I cannot doubt that a glorious discovery in natural knowledge and of the power and wisdom of God in creation is awaiting our age . . .'

It is a prophet's proclamation, but I think that he himself had already made a great part of that 'glorious discovery'.

Imagination is essential in a research worker and Faraday had a soaring imagination. He once described himself when a young apprentice as 'a very lively imaginative person', who, 'could believe in the *Arabian Nights* as easily as in the *Encyclopedia*; but facts were important to me and saved me. I could trust a fact.' For Faraday the way of scientific advance was always this: his imagination conceived a hypothesis which he tested by experiment; when the evidence of his experiments harmonized with theory, then he felt himself close to truth. But at all steps there was the possibility of error. He viewed the power of the imagination with caution; as he pointed out: 'Man's natural mind is a very unstable thing and most credulous. The imagination often rules it when reason ought to be there. Mesmerism has great power over it; so has poetry; so has music. . .' Indeed the senses may even deceive themselves over the facts. As Faraday once wrote in a letter to his brother-in-law, Edward Barnard:

. . . in all kinds of knowledge I perceive that my views are insufficient and my judgment imperfect. In experiments I come to the conclusions which, if partly right, are sure to be in part wrong; if I correct by other experiments, I advance a step, my old error is in part diminished, but is always left with a tinge of humanity, evidenced by its imperfection . . . In affairs of life 'tis the same thing . . .'

Everything must be subjected to the judgement and every conclusion depends on it. It was a quality, Faraday felt, in which his confident Victorian world was rather lacking. It was part of Faraday's humility to be so conscious of the inevitability of human error.

Faraday's caution about the power of the imagination does not mean that he did not speculate; but he put firm limits on it. At the end of a letter describing far-reaching ideas he writes:

I think it likely that I have made many mistakes in the preceding pages, for even to myself my ideas on this point appear only as the shadow of a speculation, or as one of those impressions on the mind which are allowable for a time as guides to thought and research. He who labours in experimental inquiries knows how numerous these are, and how often their apparent fitness and beauty vanish before the progress and development of real natural truth.

Theory, he held, was only a temporary vehicle for truth. In his papers describing new work he relied as far as possible on facts rather than theory to gain acceptance of his results. The story he had to tell was strange to his generation of philosophers, but they had to accept his facts; he did not care that his theories were not generally understood, they could wait, but all the same he employed tact by explaining them as far as possible in the language of current thinking, which helped towards their acceptance.

While Faraday was still an apprentice there was a group of brilliant young scientists and mathematicians up at Cambridge: Herschel, Babbage and Airy among them. All three were undergraduates in 1811. Later they became Faraday's friends, his admirers and critics; but Faraday was never one of a band with his contemporaries in science. Perhaps his origins were too different, and his training; he had had to run so fast to catch up to where they started. Perhaps Sandemanian seclusion kept him a bit apart. He worked alone and liked it so. Perhaps he could not share with others his daring hope. My father W.H. Bragg once wrote of the research worker in awe before his vision, appalled and humble before his task, that such a one would rather start on his work alone. Even a child will say 'don't look' as he attempts some feat for the first time. No student ever helped Faraday, no band of research workers gathered as disciples round their prophet; there is no record of Faraday working other than alone, save for the staunch Anderson. Not that any RI professor ever captained a team of workers at the Institution during the 19th century; teams and grants to support them are things of the 20th.

Faraday sought to save all his energy for his work and desired only to be left alone to get on with it, but in the 1820s other scientists were restive. There was a general feeling that something was wrong with British science; Herschel, the great astronomer, lamented, and the explosive Babbage was spoiling for a fight. The Royal Society was the point of attack. In 1830 Babbage published a fiercely critical book, *Reflections on the Decline of Science in England*. He accused the Universities of not teaching and the State of not supporting pure science. He compared British science unfavourably with science on the Continent, and lashed the Royal Society. Faraday thought that Babbage's attack was unwarranted and his words exaggerated, and for once he looked up from his laboratory bench and made protest. He published at his own expense the translation of a pamphlet written by a Dutchman, Moll, *On the Alleged Decline of Science in England by a Foreigner*. Moll defended English science, and was against the specialization that Babbage admired in France and against the appointment of scientists to government positions. It is easy to see how Faraday, with his feeling for 'generalization' and the unity of the whole, and his belief that the man of science's place was in his laboratory, should disagree with Babbage and uphold Moll.

On the other hand, Faraday agreed with the reformers where it was a question of the Royal Society. There reform *was* wanted; the old idea of science needing the patronage of the aristocracy had lingered on and the Society had too many Fellows who, though distinguished in their own right, were only indifferently interested in science. Banks had ruled for so long, and Davy, succeeding him, had not made substantial changes. By 1830 men of science were growing to professionalism and wanted *the* scientific Society to be theirs and under their control. There was an attempt to get Herschel elected President when Davy retired in 1826, but it miscarried and a Royal Duke (of Sussex) was elected instead. This spurred the reformers into action and they decided to form a new Society, all their own. In 1831 The British Association for the Advancement of Science was born. The Association was to be the mouthpiece for science; it was to catch the attention of the nation, stimulate research and provide a meeting ground for discussion. British science had been in a muddle. The British Association would put things right and repair the defects its founders saw in the Royal Society. The 'British Ass', as it came to be nick-named, was to meet annually and has done so ever since, meeting each year in a different centre. It is nice to think that the new professional society was launched from the platform of the old amateur interest, the Yorkshire Philosophical Society, and that the BA proposed a link with the amateur societies by suggesting lines of enquiry to follow and data that could be usefully collected by their members; it was a sensitive gesture, and good natural-history work was done. There was a discussion over women being allowed to join, but Dean Buckland, the President of the BA in 1832 objected that women 'would at once turn the thing into a sort of Albemarle Street dilettante meeting', which was not polite to the RI.

The BA was immediately and immensely popular. It gave the scientists a chance to meet, read papers and discuss (only lately has there been any general discussion at the Royal Society); and it was an annual Science Festival which for a time drew in the interested amateur, as music festivals do today. The BA was Science's big bid to become part of the intellectual culture of the nation, but in that it has failed to realise its founders' hopes. However, when I went with my family to BA meetings a century after it was founded, it was still a cheerful annual gathering for the scientific world and the President's speech made the headlines in the national press.

Though sympathetic to its founding, Faraday took small part in the organization of the BA; occasionally he went to meetings, but for personal reasons. He was a private person, and always he saved himself for his work. In 1827 he had refused a professorship at London University and later declined the Presidency of the Royal Society and also of the Royal Institution. He refused a knighthood; he preferred to remain plain Michael Faraday, natural philosopher, in his laboratory.

Still less did Faraday take any part or interest in politics. He remarked in his journal on the Continental Tour: 'Tuesday March 7 1815. I heard news that Bonaparte was again at liberty. Being no politician, I did not trouble myself much about it, though I suppose it will have strong effect on the affairs of Europe.' Faraday was mildly conservative, believing that, on the whole, things are best left as they are; radical change and especially the radical spirit abroad in 1848 left him cold. He wrote in 1849 to his friend Professor de la Rive in Geneva, 'For me, who never meddle with politics and who think very little of them as one of the games of life, it seems sad that Scientific men should be so disturbed by them, and so the progress of pure . . . philosophy be much and so often disturbed by the passions of men.'

In Faraday's letters contemporary events find little or no mention. One would have thought that the Institution might have played some part in or had some link with the 1851 Exhibition, for the Prince Consort was friend to Faraday and the RI; but apart from one reference to 'this year of our great exhibition' I have found nothing in his letters.

But Faraday was a loyal subject, and it was a different matter when the Government asked him to advise them or take on some investigation; then he was ready to put time and trouble at their disposal. In 1830 he was investigating methods of cleaning pictures in the National Gallery which were sadly affected by the smoky air of London (in Trafalgar Square water for the sparkling fountains was pumped by a steam engine belching smoke). The statues in the British Museum were begrimed and the surface of the Elgin marbles was being eaten away; Faraday shook his head, all he could advise was washing with a solution of sodium carbonate. And he was consulted about the stonework of the new Palace of Westminster already being affected by decay.

A direct development of Faraday's magnetism experiments in the 1820s was the electric telegraph. By the 1840s lines were spread over

Europe and over America, but how to link the continents? When the current passed through submarine wires the signal became fuzzy with distance. Faraday was consulted at the instigation of Airy, the Astronomer Royal, who valued swift communication for correlating astronomical observations in far distant places. Faraday analysed a 'retardation effect'; and William Thomson (later Lord Kelvin) carried forward Faraday's ideas to make the transatlantic cable a practical proposition.

But perhaps the most valuable, and the most sustained work Faraday did for the common weal was his work for lighthouses, their lights and their safety. In 1836 he accepted appointment as 'Scientific Adviser to the Corporation of the Trinity House in experiments on lights'. Oil lamps had long replaced the primitive beacon; through the fifties various improved types of light were proposed, such as lime light and magnetic electric light. These he tested, and not only for their illumination; shrewdly he considered every aspect of maintenance and the welfare of the lighthouse men. Scientific superiority was not enough. He enjoyed the work which involved visits to lighthouses and experimenting in the field as well as in the laboratory. He inspected the new lights in all weathers, fog and gale, from an open boat to test their effectiveness, and once climbed over hedge and wall in a snow-blocked landscape to reach the Dover light, when he was in his seventieth year. But after that he handed over to John Tyndall, his colleague at the R I since 1853, who was appointed to Trinity House in his stead.

Faraday, when asked for advice by the Government or other body, answered the question in strictly objective manner. For instance, during the Crimean war he was consulted about the feasibility of 'smoking out' the fort of Kronstadt with poison gas: the suggestion was for sulphur-filled ships to be set alight when the wind was in the right direction to blow clouds of sulphur dioxide into the city. Faraday said it was impossible to try out this experiment and anyway the wind might change. He did not say that it was a wicked idea; he pointed out that the proposition was not feasible.

The same attitude applied, I think, when he was called in to give expert advice on a colliery disaster (as Davy also had been called in). In 1844 a terrible explosion occurred at Haswell Colliery in Co. Durham and many men and boys were killed. The men had duly carried their Davy lamps. Faraday (with Lyell the geologist) inspected the scene and examined the lamps. The conclusion reached at the end of a long enquiry was that lamps, which were perfectly efficient in the shallow mines worked in Davy's time, were not efficient under certain conditions in deeper mines. The very success of Davy's lamp had led to greedy coal owners sinking mines to more dangerous depths. But Faraday and Lyell agreed that there had been no actual negligence over legal safety precautions on the part of the owners. Maurice Berman in his book about the RI blames Faraday for not taking issue over the moral question of the mine owners sinking their mines too deep; Faraday, he implies, was on the side of the utilitarian capitalists. Faraday, quite simply, answered the scientific question asked of him, and then contributed liberally to a widows' and orphans' fund.

It all comes down to this: Faraday did not challenge the world he lived in, except on rare occasions. One such I have mentioned, when he had published the translation of Moll's pamphlet; another occasion was when he wrote a letter to *The Times* in 1855, complaining of the filth of the river Thames. He had travelled between London and Hungerford Bridges by steamboat at low tide and had made an experiment:

The whole of the river was an opaque pale brown fluid. In order to test the degree of opacity I tore up some white cards into pieces, and then moistened them, so as to make them sink easily below the surface, and dropped some of these pieces into the water at each pier the boat came to. Before they had sunk an inch below the surface they were indistinguishable . . . when the pieces fell edgeways the lower part was hidden from sight before the upper part was under water. . . Surely the river which flows for so many miles through London ought not to be allowed to become a fermenting sewer . . .

Punch had a nice cartoon of Father Thames rising dripping with mud to receive Faraday's visiting card.

These are small exceptions to his general rule of keeping apart from causes and campaigns, but there is one big one: his enthusiasm for education, and science education in particular. Faraday was an educator, he spoke out for it, and in his lectures at the RI he showed the way that science should be presented, especially how to present it to young minds. I shall return to the subject of Faraday's efforts to promote scientific education in Chapter 8. But his sole incursion into systematic instruction, after the manner of Brande's lectures, was made outside the RI. In 1829 he accepted an appointment to give twenty lectures a year to military cadets at Woolwich, to prepare them for exams. It is said he enjoyed the day out and the trip to Woolwich, and probably it did him good to escape from Albemarle Street.

So much toiling, so much far reaching thought and experimenting took their toll on Faraday's health. He had been compelled to give up work for short times as well as for one long period; as he aged his faulty memory teased him more and more. It troubled him much and in 1857 (when he was sixty-six) he wrote to a friend:

I am in town and at work more or less every day. My memory wearies me greatly in working; for I cannot remember from day to day the conclusions I come to, and all has to be thought out many times over. To write it down gives no assistance, for what is written down is itself forgotten. It is only by very slow degrees that this stage of mental muddiness can be wrought either through or under; nevertheless, I know that to work somewhat is far better than to stand still, even if nothing comes of it.

Faraday was so patient even with his own disabilities; but it was a patience forged by humility on strong feelings. When Lord Melbourne offered him a Civil List pension and spoke derogatively of honours for scientists and literary men as a piece of humbug (so Bence Jones writes), Faraday walked out of the room. However, kind friends on both sides came to the rescue, and Faraday accepted an apology and the pension. Mrs Faraday must have been relieved.

Sarah Faraday stayed in the background of her husband's life, and made that background happy. He was devoted to her. One day when they were just engaged he wrote: 'What can I call myself to convey most perfectly my affection and love for you? Can I, or can truth, say more than for this world I am yours?'

And another letter, headed 'Royal Institution, Tuesday evening', is touchingly human and endearing:

I have been thinking all the morning of the very delightful and interesting letter I would send you this evening, and now I am so tired, and yet have so much to do, that my thoughts are quite giddy and run round your image without any power of themselves to stop and admire it. I want to say a thousand kind, and believe me, heartfelt things to you, but am not master of words fit for the purpose; and still as I ponder and think on you, chlorides, trials, oil, Davy, steel miscellanea, mercury, and fifty other professional fancies swim before me and drive me further and further into the quandary of stupidness!

He wrote this in 1820. Over forty years later it is the same simplicity of devotion in a letter from Dungeness which starts, 'Here at the lighthouse at 10 o'clock PM', and ends, 'Remember me; I think as much of you as is good either for you or me. We cannot well do without each other.' She supported him and when he was growing old, with memory fading, he sent a letter from Glasgow saying lovingly: 'The thoughts of my return to *our home* crowd in strongly upon my mind', but sadly, .'. . .my recollection rapidly fails, even as regards the friends that are in the room with me. You will have to resume your old function of being a pillow to my mind, and a rest, a happy-making wife.'

When we remember what Faraday did for the world we should think of Mrs Faraday's part in enabling him to do it. She knew when to persuade him off to the country or the sea for a rest. (Once when it rained very much, Faraday drew squares on a piece of paper and they played draughts with pink and white lozenges.) Faraday always beat her at games of skill (so a niece records) but sometimes at the RI they played bagatelle and then Mrs Faraday beat him. Games and the company of young people and family friends were his relief from work and tension, and on quiet evenings Faraday probably made the scrap books that the Institution possesses; he stuck interesting letters and cuttings into big books, with lithographs and engravings for illustrations. A number of the engravings bear the name Hullmandel, lithographer; the Faradays used to go to evening parties at the Hullmandel house, in Great Marlborough Street (quite handy to the RI) where they met the art world and musicians and singers. Faraday came to know Turner there.

By 1860 Faraday was getting too tired, too troubled in recollection to feel he could go on longer at the Institution. John Tyndall, who had been Professor of Natural Philosophy since Brande retired, was eminently capable of taking over; they had worked side by side for six years and Tyndall had proved himself both as researcher and lecturer. The Queen had given the Faradays a 'Grace and Favour' house at Hampton Court in 1858 where they had spent summer months; to Hampton Court they retired finally in 1861.

It was a pleasant house, on the Green, and there Faraday lived in sweetness of mind, accepting his fading – 'My words totter [he wrote to a friend] my memory totters and now my legs have taken to tottering and I am altogether a very tottering and helpless thing' – lovingly looked after by his wife and niece.

When I was young I knew an elderly gentleman, Sir Alfred Yarrow, the shipbuilder. When he was a boy he had heard Faraday lecture, and he would relate how he and his friends used to wait at the corner of the street to have a word with the old Professor on his way to church; and then, letting him proceed, run by a back way to intercept him at another corner, where they would receive another kindly greeting, for by then the Professor had forgotten that he had met them before.

One day a visitor to Hampton Court asked Faraday how he was. 'Just waiting,' he answered. At the end of August 1867 Michael Faraday died quietly in his chair.

FOUR

Professionalism
and Dividing Streams

JOHN TYNDALL

AROUND 1850 the Institution was going through an important change, one might say the third in its life. The first came after Rumford left in 1802, and the second in 1810 when the proprietorial character of the Institution was brought to an end. The seed for a third change sprouted in the laboratory. Through the years when hundreds of analyses were done to order and 'useful' investigations were carried out, pure research grew up until it was like a tree overshadowing other interests. The success of Davy and the awe-inspiring researches of Faraday compelled respect for experimental philosophy as an end in itself.

The position of the RI needed clarifying, and in 1849 Faraday had summed up what he considered should be the Institution's aims:

1 'The RI's scientific reputation'. The Institution must hold the high place it had won in British science.
2 The RI should provide lectures acceptable to most of its Members.
3 'Advancement of Science for its own sake, i.e. without reference to its result in character or its acceptance by a sufficient number of Members in the form it may for the time assume' (Faraday's words): which meant freedom and independence for the Professors in their research, and a claim for its importance.

In 1851 a new 'Prospectus' was drawn up and in it Faraday's third aim is put first, 'To further scientific research'. This is the new conception; the third big change in the life of the RI was this change of emphasis in its aims. Scientific research had previously been looked on mainly as a means to useful ends, and this had been so not only at the RI but in the country generally. There is a letter from Liebig written to Faraday in 1844 after visiting England where he says 'What struck me most in England was the perception that only those works which have a practical tendency awaken attention and command respect, while the

Michael and Sarah Faraday (see p. 79)

John Tyndall by G. Richmond
(see p. 70)

Thomas Huxley lecturing: *Punch* cartoon by H. Furniss, 1885

purely scientific, which possess far greater merit, are almost unknown.' At the RI pure research had been less the business than the private venture of the Professors. From mid-century onward, pure science would be no longer the hand-maid but the mistress of the establishment; but not without initial tension. A thread of jealousy appeared at once and in 1852 the Prospectus was slightly but significantly altered: the first aim was re-stated as 'To promote Science and Literary Research' (literary having the connotation of 'learned' rather than its modern specialized meaning). One is glad that width of interest was insisted on.

The RI was fortunate to have among its Managers at this time a man of great vigour and personality, Henry Bence Jones. He was a physician and a chemist who had learned his chemistry in Germany like so many other English chemists, studying under Liebig himself. He knew men, understood the society of his day and was friend and medical adviser to a whole group of leading scientists. The RI owes much to his guiding hand first as Manager and after 1860 as Secretary. And it was Bence Jones who was instrumental in getting Tyndall to the RI when Brande retired.

Travelling in Germany in 1852, Bence Jones heard of the interesting work the young Irishman John Tyndall had been doing at Marburg, carrying further Faraday's investigations into the magnetic and dia-magnetic properties of bodies. Tyndall got his FRS for this work that same year (the RS was now electing young scientists). Back in England Tyndall met Bence Jones and was introduced to other RI people at a dinner party given by Sir James Clark, the Queen's physician. No doubt Tyndall talked well – he usually did – and the result was that Bence Jones organised an invitation to Tyndall to give first a Discourse and then a course of four afternoon lectures at the RI. The Discourse was given in February 1853 and was a great success. Within a few months Tyndall was appointed Professor of Natural Philosophy, and the ageing Faraday and he were established as colleagues.

Change of viewpoint at the RI reflected a general though gradual change in the position of science: science was becoming professional. It was after a long apprenticeship that Faraday had won through to the status of a professional scientist; Tyndall determinedly started at the RI as the professional, and refused to do the analyses and investigations to order, such as Faraday had worked at patiently for so long. Research and lecturing henceforward were recognised as a full-time job and, with the direct teaching of Professor Brande at an end after nearly forty years, the RI was confirmed in its new outlook, with the new Prospectus to point the way.

Though Tyndall had never served an apprenticeship as assistant at the RI, like Davy and Faraday, he had had a tough training elsewhere. John Tyndall was born in 1820 in Co. Carlow. His portrait reminds one of the long faced men you see mooning at street corners in a south of Ireland country town, and Tyndall was as ready to burst into argument, to spin a tale and extrapolate; but he had in him a hard core, a devotion to scientific truth. At a National school he acquired mathematics and a love of English language. Growing up, he used his mathematics in surveying for the Ordnance Survey at Youghal, and his love of words in discussion of politics and religion and in writing articles for newspapers. He got a job in an engineering firm at Manchester and surveyed for railway construction, working frantically in the days of the railway race. Normally he worked nine or ten hours a day, but on one occasion there was a fearful crescendo when the plans for a projected line had to be deposited in London by noon on a certain day (30 November 1844); Tyndall and his team worked all through the night and the plans were got to London on time by special train steaming at full speed. It was in these days that he formed a life-long friendship with Thomas Archer Hirst the mathematician. Hirst's Journal and the letters they exchanged tell much about Tyndall: biographers can be thankful for Victorian journals and the lack of telephones.

In 1847 Tyndall turned schoolmaster and went to teach mathematics at a unique school, Queenwood, near Stockbridge in Hampshire, the first school in England to adopt practical and laboratory work in the teaching of applied science, which included engineering and farming. The school took forty farm pupils. But Tyndall not only taught; he learned. He encountered natural philosophy for the first time, and learned geology, botany, hydrostatics and heat, also chemistry from a man called Frankland who later in 1862 became a Professor at the RI. Sir Edward Frankland is remembered for being one of the founders of synthetic organic chemistry and a pioneer in the purification of sewage, that urgent subject in which Dewar also became involved years later. 'Chemistry is beginning to be more beautiful as I attain to a clearer vision of it,' wrote Tyndall from Queenwood, though later his mathematics would draw him more towards physics as he employed the means of the one to explore the problems of the other.

Tyndall also learned German, so that in spite of financial difficulty he was persuaded (by Frankland) to go and study chemistry in Germany, at Marburg, under the great German chemist Bunsen. Tyndall has described Bunsen as 'the ideal university teacher'. The young Irishman was delighted and deeply impressed by Marburg University and denied himself sleep to get through his work and obtain a degree before his money ran out. There he did the excellent piece of research that brought him to Bence Jones's notice and so to the RI.

The new Professor started at the Institution in September 1853 on a very small salary; that season he gave nineteen lectures there on Heat, and six at the London Institution on Electricity and Magnetism. He was living on a shoestring and overworked enthusiastically, eking out his salary by writing and examining. After four years Faraday got Tyndall's lecture load reduced, and Bence Jones did all he could to promote his research. He knew that it was only the opportunities for research that could hold a man at the RI on so small a salary when he could earn much more by teaching elsewhere, though Tyndall certainly appreciated the opportunity of lecturing to the intellectual élite at the RI and the contacts with them which he made there.

Tyndall had experienced the German system of education. In a letter written from Marburg in 1848 he had written, 'During the semester everybody [here] seems to be gathering knowledge; it will take years of devoted effort to bring England up to the same standard.' He had been a schoolmaster in Hampshire and what he observed in Germany made him an educator for life. A few years later he is still complaining: 'The natural sciences are in a sad mess in England. People appear to have no clear idea what the region of physics is.' He himself defined physics in an 1854 lecture as occupying a place midway between astronomy and chemistry.

But the confusion as subjects separated out (defining their boundaries as robins sing in autumn to define their territory) was as nothing to the confusion caused by the lack of system in the teaching of science and in English education generally, so unlike the ordered system in Germany that Tyndall so much admired. Education was a burning question during the second half of the 19th century and the RI, through its professors Faraday and Tyndall, was naturally involved. I have written about this in Chapter 8. Here I want first to tell of the relationship between the two men, and of the RI in the years they worked alongside each other, before Faraday retired to Hampton Court and

Tyndall became resident Professor in his stead; and then to tell something of Tyndall's scientific achievements at the Institution.

Tyndall and Faraday were so different in temperament, as different as Faraday was from Davy. Perhaps they got on so well just because they were different, because Tyndall loved and revered Faraday, and because Faraday had disciplined himself to a saint-like patience. Tyndall's admiration of the older man was near worship. Here is his description of Faraday giving his 1854 lecture on 'Mental Education'. It was 'such a lecture as seldom falls to the lot of man to hear . . . At intervals you could feel his powerful spirit as it glowed underneath his utterance and made it deep and musical, while the audience seemed lifted by a billow and held suspended between earth and heaven. He had nothing to do but to hold on to the riches of his own mental experience . . .' Everyone who has described Faraday lecturing speaks of him in 'glowing' terms.

But Tyndall could disagree with Faraday the scientist. There is spicy excitement to a young man in criticizing the views of the sage; Faraday himself, when lecturing to the City Philosophical Society as a very young man, had dared to criticize the electrical theories of the day. Tyndall records a conversation with Faraday about some diamagnetism work on which they held different views: 'I told him that we [Tyndall and his co-worker at Marburg] felt compelled to differ from him'. 'No matter,' replied Faraday, 'you differ not as a partisan, but because your conviction compels you.' And Faraday's reaction was the same after a lecture of Tyndall's at the R I. Tyndall describes, 'Though my aim and object in that lecture was to subvert the notions of Faraday . . . it was very far from producing in Faraday either enmity or anger . . . At the conclusion of the lecture he quitted his accustomed seat, crossed the theatre to the corner in which I had shrunk, shook me by the hand and brought me back to the table.' But then Faraday always was prepared to wait for truth to be established, prepared to find himself wrong. Tyndall, in the heat of discussion, always knew himself to be right; but he shared with Faraday respect for natural law and the verdict of experiment. Actually both were right in this particular instance.

So Faraday won the heart of the difficult moody Tyndall. But the latter, though he might be right in correcting details of some of Faraday's work, never deeply understood Faraday's vision and theories; he could not see so far. Writing to his friend Hirst in 1855

Tyndall speaks almost condescendingly: 'Many write to Faraday asking what the lines of force are. He bewilders even men of eminence . . . and if you look for exact knowledge in his theories you will be disappointed – flashes of wonderful insight you meet here and there, but he has no exact knowledge himself, and in conversation he readily confesses this.' Tyndall, trained on mathematics, is being a little superior – people who can do sums often are. Faraday, however, writing, a bit defensively but rather pleased about some result, to his friend Richard Phillips in 1831, makes the remark that, 'It is quite comfortable to me to find that experiment need not quail before mathematics, but is quite competent to rival it in discovery.' Faraday used as little mathematics as possible. A friend (Mrs Crosse) records that Faraday once remarked to her, 'It is a matter of serious régret to me that I am no mathematician; if I could live my life again, I would study mathematics; it is a great mistake not to do so, but it is too late now.' It was Clerk Maxwell who later explained Faraday's theories mathematically, turning his insights into exact mathematical statements and paving a way for further advance.

I have said that Faraday and Tyndall were different; temperamentally they were poles apart. Faraday had a serenity derived from the sure anchor of his religious faith which he did not talk about; Tyndall was questing, restless, ever ready to argue about religion and write about science and religion. Faraday kept apart from the burning questions of evolution and I have found no mention of Darwin or *The Origin* in his letters or writing. Tyndall threw himself into Darwinian controversy – or any other, though in rushing to defend a cause he could go too far and start fresh war; he was frequently in trouble. At a meeting of the British Association at Glasgow in 1855 Tyndall's feelings got badly hurt. Faraday wrote on 6 October 1855, to smooth him down. It is such a wise and revealing letter that I quote at length from it.

I was put into a very mixed mind by your last letter; glad to hear from you, that you were out of the turmoil . . . but sorry for some annoyance which I saw you had met with at Glasgow. These great meetings, of which I think very well altogether, advance science chiefly by bringing scientific men together, and making them to know and be friends with each other; and I am sorry when that is not the effect in every part of their course. I know nothing except from what you tell me, for I have not yet looked at the report of the proceedings, but let me as an old man, who ought by this time to have profited by experience, say that, when I was younger I often misinterpreted the intentions of people, and found that they did not mean what at the time I supposed they meant; and further, that as a general rule it was better to be a little dull of apprehension when phrases seemed to imply pique, and quick in perception when, on the contrary, they seemed to convey kindly feeling. The real truth never fails ultimately to appear, and the opposing parties are, if wrong, sooner convinced when replied to forbearingly, than when overwhelmed. All I mean to say is, that it is better to be blind to the results of partisanship and quick to see goodwill. One has more happiness in oneself in endeavouring to follow the things which make for peace. You can hardly imagine how often I have been heated in private when opposed, as I have thought unjustly and superciliously, and yet have striven and succeeded, I hope, in keeping down replies of a like kind; and I know I have never lost by it. I would not say all this to you if I did not esteem you as a true philosopher and friend.

In their home and social lives also, there was such difference between the two men: Faraday was complete and content, with Sarah for peace and understanding, nieces and young people around for laughter; Tyndall was a bachelor for many years and hungry for many things. Faraday chose seclusion for the sake of his work; Tyndall sought social life, not as Davy had done for status and glitter but because he was lonely. Doors opened readily for him, for Tyndall was eloquent, and there was always the chance of an exciting argument when he was a dinner guest. Davy had moved in the titled circles of the landed aristocracy, while Tyndall's circle was an intellectual aristocracy, the new professionals mingling with the old cultured upper class. Davy's circle were excited about science and hoped to get something out of it, but Tyndall's friends were interested in science for its own sake. They were the new intelligentsia.

The first half of the 19th century was the last period when men of culture could hope to understand something of most subjects; already the different disciplines were separating out and specialist societies were proliferating. The Linnean had been founded as far back as 1788, the Geological (which Davy had wanted to keep as a dining club) in 1807; Davy secured a grant of land in Regents Park, and the Zoological Society was founded in 1826, the Astronomical in 1820, the Geographical in 1830. The Royal Society itself, after the reform of its statutes in 1847, was becoming a more strictly scientific society to which it was the highest scientific honour to be elected. When old Sir Henry Holland in his *Recollections of Past Life* complained of 'the extravagant multiplication of societies of every kind, dividing all the concerns of human life', he was looking back from the 1870s over an inevitable trend as knowledge increased. It was a stimulating time with the new growth of science springing up through the old learning. Men could still understand each other enough to criticize and collaborate, and one subject fertilized another. Men of culture might belong to several societies, according to their several interests.

Among the RI Managers W.R. Hamilton, the Treasurer from 1832–49, was a travelled diplomat, interested in science and a founder of the Geographical Society. Henry Holland, President of the RI, was an enthusiastic traveller and antiquary, interested in scientific medicine and in everybody titled and eminent (his memoirs are fascinating). The Secretary of the Institution from 1843–60 was John Barlow, a parson who wrote on physiology and insanity. It shows the trend of the times that Barlow, the amateur of science, was succeeded as Secretary by the highly professional physician Henry Bence Jones – although he, too, had good knowledge of chemistry.

Looking through the Members' lists at the RI one sees what a variety of people the Institution attracted. Most of the well-known names in mid-Victorian London are there; they came to find out what was going on in the world of learning, and some of the less distinguished came to sit beside the great. Chantrey the sculptor was a Member in the forties, and artists joined, interested in the chemistry of pigments; Eastlake, the President of the Royal Academy, consulted Faraday on fresco colours in 1844. Later Fox Talbot, whose photography was going to have such an effect on art, did some of his experimenting in the RI laboratory. In 1864 Ruskin became a Member; with his ideal of 'Truth to Nature' he applauded the fine observation of science. Science, indeed, was acknowledged as 'Handmaid of the Arts'. Architects joined: Sir Charles Barry and Decimus Burton were Members. There were antiquaries and diplomats and literary ladies; among the ladies Miss Swanwick, who helped to found Girton College Cambridge and Somerville Hall Oxford, and the philanthropist Baroness Burdett Coutts, a real friend of Faraday's. The philosophic radicals were represented by a network of Darwins and Wedgwoods and Galtons, and the Christian Socialists by F.D. Maurice and Lushington the judge (both prominent at the newly founded Working Men's College). Members often joined because their friends belonged, and they brought their sisters and their cousins and their aunts. Charles Kingsley lectured; he did not belong, but his brother was a Life Member. Pusey the Oxford theologian came to listen, and Tennyson. Of course many scientists of the day belonged or came to visit the RI and its laboratory, the Institution's glory.

The late fifties and sixties were a golden period for the RI. Membership increased, lectures were crowded as the intelligentsia came to listen to scientific discovery and a wide variety of other subjects, plain instruction a thing of the past. The RI had an international reputation and its *Proceedings* were sent across the world. Research flourished with three Professors – the ageing Faraday, Tyndall and Frankland, Professor of Chemistry from 1863–8 and an old friend of Tyndall's from Queenwood days – and three assistants to help them in the laboratory. This was the one moment in the 19th century when a real 'school of research' might have developed at the Institution; but Faraday retired to Hampton Court in 1861, Frankland resigned in 1868, and money was fatally short. In 1861 Bence Jones had made a report on 'The Past Present and Future of the Royal Institution', containing an urgent appeal for financial support – 'I ask no subsidy for the RI from the Government, but I appeal, by sixty years of facts, to the Public for whose good this Institution was founded.' The Government were beginning to give grants through the newly founded Department of Science and Art, and since 1849 the Royal Society itself had been receiving £1000 a year from the Government to disburse. But the RI was too proud, too independent to accept a grant; a character it would long keep. It would have seemed like accepting charity or receiving a tip. So opportunity for building a research school was lost, and Tyndall was left a lone professor in the laboratory, like his predecessors. Even Bence Jones's private Donation Fund was not very popular with the members and was closed in 1872. But Bence Jones did get a new laboratory built and equipped for Tyndall.

Faraday's researches had set a standard and Tyndall must have felt a responsibility weighing on him. It is more than time to give some account of Tyndall's scientific achievement. It can only be a brief sketch, for this story is more about the crucial position held by the Royal Institution as an index of the waxing and waning of general regard for science and the men who were scientists, than about what they discovered.

Curiously enough, Tyndall's first essay into research was on an early line of Davy's; he experimented at Queenwood on nitrous oxide and anaesthesia. His next research at Marburg followed up Faraday's subject of diamagnetism, and this he continued in his first few years at the RI. In 1854 he gave his first Bakerian lecture at the Royal Society, 'On the nature of the forces by which bodies are repelled from the poles of a magnet'. It lasted two hours. Out of the diamagnetism work came interest in the effects of pressure; he studied the cleavage of slate in the Penrhyn quarries of N. Wales, slate being layered mud under the pressure of ages of time. He had encountered problems of pressure in his work for the railways, and he examined layers of many different kinds, including puff pastry! Thomas Huxley was present at Tyndall's RI lecture on Cleavage in 1856, and suggested studying the laminated structure of ice in glaciers; so Tyndall read *Travels through the Alps of Savoy* by J.D. Forbes, who had done a lot of work on glaciers. Tyndall queried some of Forbes's findings and decided to go to Switzerland to investigate for himself. He visited the Rhone valley, and a new world was opened to him.

Switzerland was discovered by the English in the 19th century. Mountains were no longer a horrid barrier but sublime, and mountaineering became a craze. Tyndall was unlucky not to reach the summit of the Matterhorn before Whymper conquered it in 1865; there is still 'Pic Tyndall' on the Italian ridge. With the Huxleys, Tyndall scrambled on glaciers and, walking in the mountains, encountered other English visitors: the Hookers from Kew and Henslows from Cambridge. It was to Switzerland that the Faradays went for three months after the Professor's breakdown in health in the forties. As a mountaineer Tyndall loved Switzerland passionately for the rest of his life, going there every summer, and later when married he built a chalet at Bel Alp above Brig.

After much measuring of glaciers and watching change from one season to the next, Tyndall evolved the theory that it was pressure that determined the structure of their movement. He later published a very popular book, *Glaciers of the Alps*, which involved him in controversy with Professor Forbes. Out of glacier research grew his work on radiation and absorption of heat by gases and vapours, for he noted the abnormal temperature conditions at high altitudes; he established the part that water vapour played in conserving the sun's heat at the surface of the earth. The subject of heat occupied him and in 1858 he gave a famous course of lectures at the RI, 'Heat considered as a Mode of Motion'. He was fussed and tired and in poor condition at the time, but Mrs Faraday tried to bolster him up with a good meal before each lecture. They appeared in book form in 1863 with a second edition in 1865.

Glancing at Tyndall's subjects through a lifetime of research they seem at first sight so varied: heat (Rumford's old subject) and cold, pressure, and gaseous radiation – but each always grew out of the one before. Only his excursion into biology seems a big leap, but that too sprang from the radiation work, and with it Tyndall made perhaps his greatest contribution to science.

For his radiation experiments Tyndall needed to prepare air that was free from any suspended matter for mixing with his gas. This led him to study the motes in air, and to decide that it was the scattering of light by fine particles suspended in it that makes the sky look blue. Next he began to think about the part that dust in the air played in spreading bacterial infection. He began experimenting in the early seventies and became convinced that the dust in the air contained living spores. In 1875–6 he was busy making soups; he sealed sterilized soups in test tubes and established that they remained unchanged till the tubes were opened and the soup exposed to the air, when bacterial spores in the air had access and moulds began to grow. The RI preserves to this day tubes of hare, chicken and meat broths in perfect condition that Tyndall sealed up over a century ago.

During the 1860s and 1870s, Pasteur in France was working out the germ theory of disease, and Lister in England, inspired by Pasteur's work, was developing the principles and methods of antiseptic surgery. Tyndall's investigations interlocked with their work; between them they proved conclusively that putrefaction was due to spores in the air and that life cannot spring from no-life. The myth of spontaneous generation was killed at last.

Tyndall became Resident Professor when Faraday retired, and he was lonely in the flat. He was sought after and had friends in plenty; he might dine at lordly tables or discuss with the best minds of the age at the Metaphysical Society, including F.D. Maurice, Ruskin, Manning and Gladstone. He visited Tennyson at Farringford where Tennyson read 'Maud' to him (he loved reading Maud) and they looked through Tennyson's telescope. He enjoyed companionship with the younger scientists as a member of the X Club, with Huxley, Lubbock, Hirst; they had cheerful parties that included wives and once went on a picnic to Epping Forest and climbed trees. But in spite of all this, he suffered.

He suffered from overwork, indigestion, doubt and depression. In short he lacked a wife. After an abortive attempt to engage one young lady, he met another, Louisa Hamilton, in 1872. Louisa had been brought to RI lectures by her mother, Lady Claud Hamilton (Lady Palmerston used to bring her daughters; indeed it was quite a thing for intellectual mothers to bring daughters to lectures and this went on into my own time at the RI – but one does not recognise them there now). Tyndall met the Hamiltons again in the summer in Switzerland, and in 1876 there followed an engagement. John was 56, Louisa 31; she became his adoring wife, amanuensis and ministering angel. Wives of eminent men have a great responsibility and, in the 19th century especially, were inclined to adore and smother. Wordsworth had a sister as well as a wife to watch over him; Tennyson had Emily, who spoiled him but must have had a sense of humour because Edward Lear was so fond of her. But I think Sarah Faraday must have been the perfect companion and wife.

Tyndall needed someone to laugh at and with him; he thought too much about himself, but then he slept badly and had a poor digestion. Louisa may have spoiled him, but it was a good marriage and they lived happily and cheerfully together all his days. Alas they had no children. No Resident Professor had a child during the first 125 years of the Institution's history.

The mid-Victorians, the society in which the Tyndalls lived, enjoyed a proud confidence; the 1851 Exhibition demonstrated it. There seemed no end to what science might discover and machinery achieve. Confidence bred belief in freedom, free trade, free enterprise; and for the first half of the century these Victorians had complete confidence in their view of the Truth. In England science and religion were still marching together; God had created the world and all the species in it. Science was merely uncovering God's laws; Truth was one.

But a fissure was about to widen into a crevasse: the how and when of Creation was in dispute. There were two sources of information, the Bible and Science. The traditionalists accepted the date of 4004 BC for the Creation of the world (still commonly printed in the Authorised Version when I was a child); but the date had to be put further and further back as geology propounded an ever greater age for the earth. Study of rocks and fossils showed that there simply would not have been time for so many species to grow and decay and for new ones to have been created since 4004 BC. And how had species died out? The Neptunists held that the Flood in the Bible story was only one of many; the Vulcanists held that earthquake was the destroyer; the Uniformitarians believed that changes had come about by fire *and* water, but infinitely slowly. It was Charles Lyell, the great geologist, who grasped the truth that through aeons of time change in the structure of the earth had come about by the natural forces that are still acting today.

But the generally held belief was that it was God who was continuing to create new forms of life as the old ones died out. Man was his latest creation, supreme because he had a soul and could himself both reason and create; he was made in God's image.

Then, in 1831, the young naturalist Charles Darwin went on the famous *Beagle* voyage. He took Lyell's new book, *Principles of Geology*, with him; he studied fossil bones in the Andes and every living thing he saw and came home with a conviction that it was by a long process of evolution and not by destruction and new creation that species altered or decayed. A couple of years after his return Charles read Malthus's famous *Essay on the Principles of Population*, where Malthus declared that population must ever increase unless curbed by disaster; obviously then it was the fittest who would survive. Evolution of species must come about by pressure of circumstance through long periods of time; to Darwin this was the only possible conclusion from his own observations and the work of Lyell and Malthus, but it was hard even for those friends in sympathy with him to accept. He sketched out his theory of Natural Selection in 1842, but *The Origin of Species* did not appear until seventeen years later: only A.R. Wallace, coming to the same conclusions, hurried him into print then. Darwin had hesitated to publish because he knew his theory must distress and make trouble. Perhaps his was not the greatest discovery of the century, but it was certainly the most shocking. The theory of Natural Selection seemed to be attributing to Nature the creative job that had been regarded as God's special province. Was Nature thus independent of God and therefore not under his moral law? If so, then science was not revealing God's ways but only Nature's mechanism, and so must be amoral.

It was the end of an era. There had been a sense of Unity, God-centred. Historians, theologians and natural philosophers had been able to understand each other's minds, for they shared the same approach to God's Truth, an ideal not clearly defined but known by all to be there, with Science uncovering one aspect. Now Truth was split;

science and religion seemed each to be telling a different story. The scientists themselves had to struggle to accept Darwin's conclusions; the Church retreated into its own truth and the ordinary man was sad and confused, horrified to have it pointed out that he was 'descended from an ape', and was not a special creation after all. People were left either to live with two Truths, Biblical and Scientific, keeping them as separate as possible, or they had to reject one or other, or to re-think the faith they lived by. Unity had gone and fragmentation had come in to stay.

Two of the RI professors, Tyndall and Huxley, were well involved in all the controversy (but not the aged Faraday, retired by 1861). Tyndall claimed that science should and would 'wrest from theology the entire domain of cosmological theory'. Thomas Huxley, the Fullerian Professor of Physiology for two periods, was Darwin's great protagonist and Tyndall supported him. While Darwin quietly got on with his natural history in the seclusion of Down House, Huxley fought his battles for him, speaking and lecturing. There is a letter dated 1 March 1862 from Sir W. Frederick Pollock, the barrister and staunch RI Member:

There have been some interesting lectures at the Royal Institution lately . . . one by Huxley on the presumed great antiquity of the human species . . . his demands . . . rise to hundreds, even thousands of thousands of years. Sir Charles Lyell is bringing out a book on the subject [*Antiquity of Man*] which will no doubt be chosen as a point of assault by those wise religionists who think they can separate creation from the Creator, and who choose to see danger to spiritual belief in every fresh discovery in physical science, and fancy that Truth is not in unity with itself . . .

Pollock's idea of Truth was big enough to welcome Darwin's theories; but, even when they accepted, thinking people saw in the survival of the fittest the seed of the idea of the master race, and feared it. They saw the moral consequences to minds divided by different truths. And so many nice ordinary people were made sad. Tennyson anticipated their plight when he was writing *In Memoriam* a decade or so before; all the controversy about the age of the earth caused much worry long before Darwin administered the final shock.

> I stretch lame hands of faith and grope
> And gather dust and chaff and call
> To what I feel is lord of all
> And faintly trust the larger hope

John Tyndall himself provided further shocks for the age, less devastating because delivered to a public that had been forced to try and digest *The Origin*. In a discourse given before the British Association at Liverpool in 1870 Tyndall spoke on the still smouldering question of Evolution: 'In more senses than one, Mr Darwin has drawn heavily upon the scientific tolerance of his age . . . [His] observation, imagination and reason combined have run back with wonderful sagacity and success over a certain length of the line of biological succession.' In 1873 Tyndall carried the whole discussion one most important step further back, boldly posing the question of the origin of life itself:

Does life belong to what we call matter, or is it an independent principle inserted into matter at some suitable epoch? . . . What are the core and essence of this hypothesis [of Natural Evolution]? Strip it naked, and you stand face to face with the notion that not alone the more ignoble forms of animal life, not alone the nobler forms of the horse and lion, not alone the exquisite and wonderful mechanism of the human body, but that the human mind itself – emotion, intellect, will . . . were once latent in a fiery cloud . . . [and also] all our philosophy, all our poetry, all our science, and all our art.

This was spoken to Section A (Physics) of the BA at Nottingham and is a foreshadowing of Tyndall's famous Belfast Address, next year. At Belfast (1874) he spoke as President; his words then had presidential weight and publicity and caused the more stir, second only to the 'Darwin scandal' itself. Tyndall led his hearers through the dignity of ancient thought (a tactful start before a mixed audience reared on the classics), via the ideas of Democritus, Epicurus, Lucretius, and then, passing to Bishop Butler and Darwin, Tyndall arrived at this:

By a necessity engendered and justified by science I cross the boundary of the experimental evidence and discern in that Matter which we, in our ignorance of its latent powers and notwithstanding our professed reverence for its Creator, have hitherto covered with opprobrium, the promise of all terrestrial life.

This was an uncompromising and startling statement from the man who had disproved the theory of spontaneous generation. But here is his resolution of the seeming contradiction:

They [the scientists] are intimately acquainted with the structural power of matter . . . they can justify scientifically their *belief* in its potency, under the proper conditions, to produce organisms. But . . . they will frankly admit their inability to point to any satisfactory experimental proof that life can be developed save from demonstrable antecedal life. [Properly sterilized soups in sealed tubes do *not* produce mould: Tyndall had proved it] . . . They draw the line from the highest organism through lower ones down to the lowest; and it is the prolongation of this line by the intellect, beyond the range of the senses, that leads them to the conclusion which Bruno so boldly enunciated.

In the 16th century Giordano Bruno had stated that all creation is one life composed of many living members which in their ultimate existence are eternal, and that the life animating the whole is God; for which assertion he was burnt as a heretic.

Tyndall was claiming the right of the scientific imagination to speculate beyond the range of experiment. Churchmen and theologians rose up in arms and cried out against him, but Huxley fought for Tyndall's truth. Argument went on, dragged on. In 1877 Rudolph Virchow, the great German pathologist, speaking in Munich, maintained that Evolution 'was not experimentally proved', but Tyndall defended his position, pointing out how many adherents the new theory now had. Carlyle (Tyndall's hero) at first hated Darwin's evolutionary ideas as weakening the ethical element of life, but he came round slowly.

Darwin had fragmented belief, but the new theories had to be lived with; they had come to stay. People got used to them. There was so much else to think about as the century wore on; for one thing, the great new concept of the British Empire.

After his marriage in 1876 Tyndall's life was much softened and enriched by Louisa's comforting companionship; happiness, people and plenty, visits to Scotland staying with his wife's aristocratic relations, holidays in his beloved Switzerland; life was transformed for him. The Tyndalls were hospitable, and after Friday Discourses they often entertained in their own rooms in the RI. Tyndall had the pleasure of being popular as a lecturer; with his flair for the picturesque he once lectured on rainbows wearing cape and sou'wester in an artificial shower in the lecture theatre. I fancy he enjoyed himself lecturing on Goethe's *Farbenlehre*; Goethe, not content to be a poet, would like to have been recognised as a scientist as well. He worked out his own theory of light and colour, criticizing Newton, but Tyndall said his science was unsound.

Tyndall relished telling people they were wrong. 'I trounced him', he once wrote of someone he had vanquished in a dinner party argument.

One can think of other people, great in their own sphere, who have had 'ideas' on other spheres of knowledge; the tendency is to wish they wouldn't, and try to push them back into their own compartments. Let the specialist remain a specialist in his own subject, he is more useful there: but it is a sad snub to width of knowledge.

It was a busy life for the Tyndalls at the RI, and the Professor also became involved in national utilitarian problems as had Davy and Faraday before him. In the 19th century to call in an RI professor was an obvious thing to do. In the 1870s Tyndall served on a Royal Commission on the ever recurring problem of explosions in coal mines, and on a Special Commission on lighting by electricity. His incursions into biology drew him into the campaign for public health, backing Huxley's efforts and advocating cleanliness in the fight against the scourge of tuberculosis (the tubercle bacillus had lately been discovered).

But all Tyndall's activities were accompanied by controversy. No sooner had he been appointed to Trinity House, succeeding Faraday in 1865, than he became embroiled in trouble over the Eddystone light. After the Belfast Address it was so often a science and religion controversy; and he spoke and he argued and he wrote, always to expose misapprehension and what he considered as error. I doubt he ever found peace of heart. He was rather fond of writing on religious subjects, and in his two volumes of essays, *Fragments of Science*, and *More Fragments*, there are three religious essays, 'Reflections on Prayer and Natural Law', 'Miracles and Special Providences', and 'On Prayer as a form of Physical Energy'. In the last he wrote: 'Religion, in fact, varies with the nature on which it falls. Often unreasonable, if not contemptible, prayer, in its purer forms, hints at disciplines which few of us can neglect without moral loss. But no good can come of giving it a delusive value by claiming for it a power in physical nature.' Tyndall would condemn praying for rain, or for a cattle plague to end. Serenity of faith was never his; but it is a religious man who will go on searching, and fighting for Truth as he sees it. Those three Resident Professors at the RI, Davy, Faraday and Tyndall, were all deeply religious men in very different ways.

All this controversy was exhausting. Tyndall continued to sleep badly and suffered from indigestion and depression in spite of his wife's cosseting. In 1881 Carlyle died, Darwin and Dean Stanley the year after; the older generation that Tyndall had looked up to were departing, and his own energetic grasp of life and problems was beginning to

Sir James Dewar

Dewar lecturing by T. Brooks, 1904 (see p. 98)

Ludwig Mond

Lord Rayleigh

slip. He thought of retirement; he and Louisa built a house up on the heights of Hindhead where the pure air reminded them of Switzerland, and later gave up their Swiss home. Whenever they could they escaped to Hindhead from the Institution which was getting more and more uncomfortable; the Managers were changing and the difficulties of co-operation with the Professor of Chemistry, James Dewar (appointed 1877), only increased as Tyndall grew less efficient and Dewar more tiresomely brilliant and competent. In 1887 Tyndall gave up the struggle and resigned. Dewar stepped briskly into his shoes to reign as Resident Professor for the next thirty-six years. In the following chapter I shall tell more about relationships between the two men, and of Tyndall's tragic death in 1893.

FIVE

Research and Decline

JAMES DEWAR

WHILE Managers have always maintained a reasoned continuity at the Royal Institution, trying to balance the Institution's aims against the need to run the club aspect efficiently, the Professors have provided the spark; especially, of course, the Professor resident at the time. The RI has taken its character from its Professors; to them it owes its reputation. So, any story about the RI has to be an account of its Professors, and biographies in quantity have been written about the earlier ones. ('Not *another* about Uncle Michael?' Faraday's close relative exclaimed to Pearce Williams who wrote the last important biography of Faraday.) I have studied these biographies gratefully.

But nobody has yet cared to write a full biography of Dewar – James Dewar, son of a Scottish Lowland publican, great chemist, brilliant experimentalist, that crusty dreamer who loved poetry, and made and played on his fiddle; who studied the sky at night through a skylight in the roof of the RI at the age of 80, invented an explosive and treasured a soap bubble. But there are letters to look at, and newspaper cuttings, and I myself listened to the Obituary lecture by Professor Henry Armstrong in 1924 (though I remember nothing of it save the lecturer's enthusiasm and fuzzy beard). I have also delved into the Managers' Minutes to extract interesting threads from the mass of facts and figures and resolutions.

To sketch something of Dewar's early life: he was born in 1842 in Kincardine on the Firth of Forth, the youngest of seven sons of an innkeeper and vintner; and like the seventh son in a fairy tale was born poor but fortunate, with clever head and skilful hands. He went to the local school, and falling through the ice on a pond one winter's day he contracted rheumatic fever which kept him away from school for many months. It is interesting and suggestive how being deprived of schooling for some considerable time has often allowed a clever child to develop in some special direction. Young James worked with the village carpenter, who must have been an extraordinary one, for under his guidance the boy learned to make fiddles. He made a fiddle for himself and learned to play it with considerable ability; he kept it all his life and it is still at the RI. When he was of an age to go to the University like all promising young Scots, he set off, not with the Scottish student's traditional bag of oatmeal, but with his fiddle under his arm – and not to be exactly a student.

Dewar went to Edinburgh University to take service with J.D. Forbes, Professor of Natural Philosophy. Forbes was friend of Whewell and Babbage and had co-operated in the founding of the British Association; it was his book *Travels in the Alps* that had started Tyndall going to Switzerland. Dewar was to prepare Forbes's lecture demonstrations and be his 'lab-boy'. But he also attended lectures and before long was taken on as demonstrator to Lyon Playfair, Professor of Chemistry. Playfair had come to Edinburgh from the Royal School of Mines in Jermyn Street, where both Tyndall and Huxley lectured to working men. Dewar never took any exams; but by 1867 he had sent his first paper to the Royal Society of Edinburgh, and by 1869 he was Lecturer, soon to become Professor, at the Royal (Dick) Veterinary College in Edinburgh. He was also assistant chemist to the Highland and Agricultural Society, travelling round giving lectures at different centres, a 'peripatetic lecturer' he called himself, in the 18th century fashion of taking science round the country.

But he was busy on chemical research at Edinburgh the while. In 1872, working on specific heat investigation, he made a vacuum jacket for his calorimeter, as heat insulation. In 1874 he wrote in collaboration with P.G. Tait a paper on 'a new method of obtaining very *perfect* vacua' (*their* title, a wording somewhat unworthy of literary men). His method included the use of coco-nut charcoal for absorbing the last traces of gases to improve the vacuum. Both his vacuum jacket and coco-nut charcoal device were put to great practical use later. He was also interested in biological subjects, and worked with Professor J.G. M'Kendrick at Glasgow, on the physiological action of light on the eye.

Dewar had published fifty scientific papers through the Royal Society of Edinburgh and the British Association by 1875, when there came a complete change in his life with his appointment as Jacksonian Professor of Natural Philosophy at Cambridge. The Chair had been endowed in 1782 under the will of a Mr Jackson, Fellow of Trinity, and the conditions of election and courses to be given had been laid down in detail. A course was to consist of thirty-six lectures a year with thirty experiments in either anatomy, animal economy, chemistry, botany, agriculture or *materia medica*, and the professor was particularly to address himself 'to that *opprobrium medicorum* called the gout, both in getting a better history of the disorder and symptoms preceding attending and following it'. Such was the compass of Natural Philosophy in the late 18th century, with medicine and the sciences closely linked.

Dewar was equipped to fulfil the requirements for biology and chemistry through his work in Edinburgh, and also agriculture through his connection with the Highland and Agricultural Society and the Veterinary College. I do not imagine he knew much about the gout, but perhaps there was not quite the same urgency to study that by the last quarter of the 19th century.

Settled in Cambridge, Dewar joined forces with Liveing, Professor of Chemistry, in a long series of spectroscopic investigations; it is possible that Liveing got Dewar appointed to the Jacksonian professorship so that they could collaborate, and in the twenty-five years following they produced no less than seventy-eight papers. But Dewar did not like Cambridge, nor the donnish college atmosphere, so that when he was offered the Professorship of Chemistry at the RI in 1877 he accepted. He had already given Friday Discourses there. The aura of Faraday graced the RI, and Thomas Young, the RI professor who established the wave theory of light, was Dewar's hero. Perhaps the subject of light with all its beauty, with all it implied, appealed to the artist in Dewar, as Young's wide culture chimed with Dewar's literary bent. But perhaps the greatest draw of all was the chance of working in the RI laboratory; experimental facilities at Cambridge were not very good, and Dewar was *par excellence* an experimenter. To discover facts always meant more to him than the theories that could be built on them.

However, he did not resign the Cambridge professorship; he held both appointments for the next forty-six years until he died, and continued working with Liveing, doing many of the experiments at the RI. It is a mark of the Managers' appreciation of Dewar that when Tyndall retired and Dewar succeeded as Resident Professor, he was allowed to continue to reside for part of each year in Cambridge according to the Jacksonian terms of office.

Dewar and Tyndall overlapped at the Institution for ten years. At first they got on well together and Dewar would dine with the Tyndalls when he came to lecture. For Dewar it must have been quite a strain holding the two appointments, and in 1880 he was considering resigning from the Jacksonian, Liveing encouraging him to do so on the grounds of health. Stress of research had its effect on all the 19th-century RI scientists; Davy fell ill, Faraday had terrible headaches, Tyndall and Dewar suffered from indigestion which made Dewar the more impatient and Tyndall moody (he suffered from insomnia as well). Perhaps working in the ill-ventilated RI basement had something to do with it: scientists were expected to experiment 'below stairs' and in odd corners. No doubt health had some influence but it was predictable that trouble would develop between two such prickly men as Tyndall and Dewar, Tyndall ageing, Dewar vigorous and assertive. By the mid-eighties Tyndall's old supporters among the Managers had mostly retired and he felt the criticism of the newcomers, especially of Bramwell, a friend of Dewar.

The final blow to Tyndall was trouble over who should give the Christmas lectures in 1887–8: Tyndall and Dewar had been giving them in alternate years, but the Managers thought Tyndall was getting past it and, though it was his turn, they invited Dewar to give them instead. Tyndall was deeply hurt and Mrs Tyndall indignant, but Dewar did not offer to withdraw. It is horrible when people lose confidence in you and think you too old. Poor Tyndall threw in his hand and resigned. Dewar was made Superintendent of the House and rather hustled the Tyndalls out of the flat (so they felt). The Dewars moved in with their beautiful possessions for the rest of his life – and spread themselves.

The Tyndalls retired to Hindhead. Tyndall still lectured and wrote and argued; indeed he took up a new form of controversy, this time political, and turned his rhetoric on Mr Gladstone whom he heartily disliked – Mr Gladstone's 'was not true liberalism'. It seemed that Tyndall never could rest quiet; and now an unexpected menace arrived to upset him – neighbours, newcomers drawn to Hindhead by Tyndall's own advocacy of the pure air. The Tyndalls planted trees and erected great screens of heather and brushwood to save their privacy. It is partly his fault that Hindhead, alas, is as it is today.

And so they lived, happy together, his health their mutual care, until one fatal night in 1893 when Louisa mistook the medicine bottles by her husband's bed and gave him an overdose of chloral. The fight to counteract the drug was unavailing. 'You have killed your John,' Tyndall said. He died the next day; and with these words in her heart

Mrs Tyndall had to live on another forty-seven years without him. In the 1920s, my father, then Resident Professor at the RI, went to visit Mrs Tyndall at Hindhead. He found a little old lady in black, and blind, so that she could not see the trees that had grown up to shut out the view and make a sad barrier round the ugly house.

When Dewar took up his appointment at the RI in 1877 he began a new series of experiments on the liquefaction of gases. That year Cailletet and Pictet in Geneva succeeded in some experiments on the liquefaction of nitrogen and oxygen. Dewar was fired to investigate himself. At a Friday Discourse in 1878 he showed Cailletet's apparatus and gave his first demonstration of liquid oxygen. He built a two-ton machine for his experiments in the basement of the RI (it was still there when the Braggs moved in to the Institution in 1923; I remember it, huge and dusty). He also installed an electric generator driven by a steam engine, thereby providing a source of electric power before the laboratories were connected to the A.C. and D.C. mains in 1892. Such a facility in the laboratory was the great attraction to Lord Rayleigh when he accepted appointment as Professor of Natural Philosophy in 1887.

Faraday himself had done much work on liquefaction, and by 1845 he liquefied all the known gases save the six 'permanent gases': oxygen, nitrogen, hydrogen, nitrous oxide, methane and carbon dioxide. Perhaps Dewar felt very close to Faraday as he proceeded to try and liquefy the gases that had been beyond the means at Faraday's disposal; it was said that Dewar used to mutter to Faraday as he worked. Indeed not long ago someone asked me if I had ever seen Faraday's ghost in the twenty years I lived at the RI, for Dewar used to be heard talking with him. The answer is no.

For this low-temperature work Dewar needed an insulated vessel to hold his liquefied gases, to stop them boiling away; he used the principle of the vacuum jacket he had made for his calorimeter in Edinburgh and made silvered vacuum vessels. Take the cover off and the stopper out of our thermos flasks and you have Dewar's vessel in principle. He tried without success to get an English manufacturer to develop his idea, and it was the industrial enterprise of Germany that first put the 'thermos' on the market.

The liquefaction of gases was a scientific fact that everyone could marvel at, whether they understood how it was done or not, and it was news. There were long columns in the newspapers, often two columns, when Dewar lectured and showed liquid air or some other gas: the RI had great publicity. Here is a report in the *Daily Chronicle* for 20 January 1894:

From floor to ceiling the building was densely packed with visitors. So great was the demand for seats that groups of people in evening dress might be seen huddled on the gangway steps and even invading the precincts of the professor's table . . . Piled up on the lecture table was a perfect forest of apparatus, and punctually at 9 o'clock the laboratory assistants bore in many flagons of that precious fluid, liquid air, of which so much has been heard of late.

Dewar regarded the liquefaction of gases less as an end in itself than as an avenue into new research, and as soon as he could obtain the liquid gas in sufficient quantity he began to explore the properties of matter at low temperatures. He studied chemical action and the strength and cohesion of materials; with J.A. Fleming (later Sir Andrew) he investigated electrical and magnetic effects; with Henri Moissan he liquefied and later solidified fluorine; with Pierre Curie he worked on the effect of extreme cold on radium emanation. Pierre Curie came over from France to work with Dewar in the RI laboratory. This low-temperature work was done through a period of about twenty years, straddling the turn of the century. Dewar had a daring imagination as an experimenter, and exquisite skill in manipulation. He used to attribute the skill of his fingers to the fiddle-making in his youth.

But the work was costly, 'tedious and costly' he once described it, and the RI's resources for research were small; yet no grants from outside were sought for, or received. The RI preserved its private independent character and supported Dewar's research by a special fund 'For Low Temperature Research', to which members contributed £5, £50 or £100, as duly recorded in the Managers' Minutes; members were proud to give, one feels, to the Institution's own special research. Dewar perpetuated this spirit of individual private research to the end of his life. In 1921, two years before he died, there was a project afoot for establishing an international low temperature research laboratory in Holland. In a letter Dewar declared that this would be 'bad for the progress of original research', and castigated the proposers of the scheme as an 'audacious scientific autocracy . . . This is not the spirit that has dominated any department of Research conducted at the RI.' But he was to be the last to hold to this tradition which for the RI became a strait jacket.

However, back in 1884, he was delighting the audiences on Friday evenings with accounts of his discoveries and with his demonstrations; he was an artist in presentation. The Prince of Wales (who had been brought to Faraday's Juvenile lectures as a small boy) took the Chair at Dewar's 1884 Discourse and watched him exhibit a foaming vessel of liquid air. By 1898 Dewar had succeeded in liquefying hydrogen, the last of Faraday's 'permanent gases' to be liquefied; he collected it in an open vessel, and the next year obtained it as thin ice in his great machine by expanding the highly compressed gas through a fine orifice. He tried to liquefy helium, but that was beyond the powers of his apparatus, as oxygen and hydrogen had been beyond Faraday's. Helium was not liquefied until twenty years later by Professor Kamerlingh Onnes in his laboratory at Leiden. For his experiments Dewar needed to create high vacua; he used the charcoal method he had written about in Edinburgh days. He found that the absorptive power of charcoal was greatly increased by extreme cold. The high vacua that can thus be obtained greatly helped the advance of atomic physics in following years.

Faraday had worked in the old basement 'Servants' Hall' of 21 Albemarle Street (the name is still on the door); Tyndall and Bence Jones together organised the construction of a new physical laboratory in the space previously occupied by Davy's mineralogical collection. But by the end of the nineteenth century the R I basement was cluttered with Dewar's heavy apparatus for liquefaction experiments, and anyway, it was dark, shut in, below street level. And then in 1894 came rescue: a new laboratory and more space for Dewar's work, but much more important than that, a new conception, new opening for British science.

Ludwig Mond was an important German industrial chemist belonging to an international Jewish family. He had been trained in the great German system of science education and had studied under Bunsen (Tyndall's professor). He was one of a number of German scientists who migrated to England, some to teach like Hofmann at the Royal College of Chemistry in London, and some to set up manufactories here. Beyer made locomotives, Siemens electrical equipment. The industrial chemists were naturally drawn to the industrial north, by the cheap coal and concentrated labour force in the swiftly growing towns. Ludwig Mond had joined with John Brunner (English-born son of a Swiss immigrant) to set up ammonia soda works in Cheshire and start the firm of Brunner Mond which developed into ICI.

In 1894 Mond made a stupendous proposal to the RI, an offer to set up a new research laboratory under the Institution's wing. At the General Monthly meeting of the Managers on 2 July Mond's proposal was read out. Mond started by recalling how, in 1843, an idea had been put forward for establishing a School of Practical Chemistry at the RI, and how Faraday and Brande had approved provided that it could be done well, but the Managers had turned down the proposition, probably for lack of space (though they may also have been thinking of the extra burden it would put on Faraday at the height of his electrical researches). However, the idea was not wasted, and the need for some such body resulted in the foundation of the Royal College of Chemistry a few years later. But the laboratories of that college (and of other schools of chemistry founded later) were devoted to the teaching of practical chemistry, and Mond pointed out that still – fifty years later – no adequate provision existed in England for carrying out independent chemical researches. It is important to realise that the RI laboratory held a unique place through most of the 19th century. The greatest scientific society, the Royal, has never had a laboratory, save at its very beginning when it did hold some simple apparatus for Fellows to use, before apparatus could be bought: the philosophers and amateur scientists expected to have their own laboratory as they would their own kitchen. This tradition of the private laboratory lingered on at least to the end of the last century, Lord Rayleigh being perhaps the last professional scientist to do major research in his own laboratory at his home, Terling.

Ludwig Mond felt there was great need for laboratory facilities in England for scientists who did not have their own.. He proposed to endow a laboratory under the aegis of the RI. What better place? When his proposal was read out, he had already bought No. 20 Albemarle Street, an 18th-century house next door to the RI. He would give this house, equip and endow it for a national laboratory. No. 20 could provide space for workers in its bedroom floors, more room for the RI library to expand across its first floor, and more room for Dewar's engines to spread through the basement.

It was a superb project, and *Nature* in an article about the new 'Davy–Faraday Laboratory', as it was to be called, pointed out that Mond was fulfilling a long existing need: the Devonshire Commission on the Universities had pleaded for such facilities for scientific investigations twenty years before, but the Government had ignored their plea. Numerous schools of chemistry had grown up, but no research laboratories.

Mond reminded the Managers that the guiding aims of the abortive scheme in 1843 had been,

1 Instruction for students
2 original research
3 help for RI professors in their own research work

A laboratory assistant was the most help the RI professors had ever had.

Although Mond had the old scheme in mind, his new laboratory would not fulfil the first aim proposed in 1843. He laid down that the 'Davy–Faraday' was *not* to be educational: original research (the second aim of the old scheme) was to be its raison d'être. The laboratory was to be free to all persons without distinction of nationality or sex: a worker might apply to come and work at the Davy–Faraday laboratory (DF for short) on his own research project for six months, a year or some such period. He must support himself, he would get no subsidy: basic apparatus would be available, but he must himself supply any special-ised piece of apparatus for his project. I have looked through a file of those early applications; the very first request to join is from a Mr J.E. Petavel who in the 1920s became the Director of the National Physical Laboratory, the long desired Government laboratory set up in 1900, four years after the DF. Henry Tizard spent a year in the DF; later he did much research in aeronautics and was Chairman of the Scientific Survey of Air Warfare in the last war. A number of good scientists spent time in the laboratory, and occasionally a young professor or science master would join to come and do some piece of research in his spare time. Workers seem mostly to have been chemists. There was quite a flutter when the first young lady was admitted in 1905 (Dr Ida Smedley). But in its first quarter-century no outstanding discovery was made, no sustained line of research was associated with its name; the DF was as temporary hotel accommodation in the careers of the scientists who passed through.

The third objective in the 1843 scheme for a school of chemistry had been to supply the RI professors with help in their research work. Mond said he could not implement this idea, though he hoped that in time others would found bursaries for this purpose. These extra bursaries never were founded.

The Resident Professor became Director when the Laboratory was opened, with great acclaim by the Press, in 1896. A 'competent chief' was appointed to supervise the daily running, a chemist from Cambridge, Dr Alexander Scott, and Dewar got on with his own research in the enlarged laboratories in the RI basement. Dewar had little to do with the DF or with Scott, and when their paths crossed, they quarrelled. It ended with Scott being 'made redundant'; he protested and there was argument and litigation, but he had to go. Scott's departure brought the DF more directly under Dewar's control (and this may have made it easier for my father when he took over in 1923 as Resident Professor in the RI and Director of the DF), but in practice Dewar had little contact with the research workers and towards the end of his time the laboratory became moribund. It would rise again like a phoenix, to new heights and in a new ethos; but that belongs to the next chapter.

Money would have a lot to do with the resurgence. It is astonishing how the RI survived on so little money in the 19th century. It is an extraordinary story of hand to mouth living, of near-bankruptcy brilliance. The Institution after all started with no endowments save the money put down by the original Proprietors in 1799, about fifty guineas apiece; and all the building and equipping had to be paid for out of this, subscriptions for the lecture courses being relied upon for daily running. In the early lavish Rumfordian beginnings, when everything was to be of the best, Young was paid £300 a year and Davy £400, which was not so bad; but soon the RI realised how poor it was, and in his first twenty years Faraday never got more than £100 a year from the Institution (his earlier wage as laboratory assistant) until in 1833 Jack Fuller's endowment of a Professorship of Chemistry gave him another £100 a year.

All through the century the Resident Professors had to supplement their incomes by taking on extra outside work. During the years when thousands of analyses were being done in the laboratory two thirds of the fees went to the Professor and one third to the RI, and the fees from Brande's medical students were divided in the same proportion. The Professors acted as industrial consultants for some time: Faraday lectured to cadets at Woolwich for many years, Tyndall examined for the Army and lectured regularly at the Royal School of Mines. The RI

Professors appeared as expert witnesses in industrial lawsuits and patent cases. This was a favourite and very profitable venue for 19th-century scientists; there were plenty of lawsuits in that time of expanding industry. Dewar became a rich man through a lucrative practice as expert witness, with all the investigations involved.

The RI was continually in financial straits. In 1816 the coal bill was paid, but it was two years overdue. In 1823 a loan of £4000, interest free, was raised from among the members; without loans and bequests the Institution could not have survived.

In 1902 Dewar made a summary of RI expenditure other than domestic and architectural.

During the whole of the 19th century the total sum spent on professional staff was £54,000 . . . The laboratory expenditure was £24,000 and the assistant salaries amounted to about £21,000. This total of £100,000 with £9580 contributed by members and friends of the Institution to the fund for exceptional expenditure on experimental research, and £9600 representing the Civil List Pension of £300 annually paid to Faraday for thirty two years, really represented the whole of the money-cost of the scientific work during one century. It works out that the cost of the scientific achievements of the RI was about £1200 a year.

This was during a century in which the purchasing power of money remained remarkably steady: truly a bargain.

The 19th century put such belief and hope in science, yet it took a long time to convince Government that it was worth investing its money in it. But the Prince Consort backed science; he was a practical and far-seeing man who had first-hand knowledge of the German system of science education and knew what it was achieving. He was also a friend of Faraday and applauded the achievements of the RI. In 1859 Prince Albert was President of the British Association and in his Presidential Address he declared:

We may be justified . . . in hoping that by the gradual diffusion of science and its increasing recognition as a principal part of our national education, the public in general . . . will more and more recognise the claims of science . . . so that [science] will speak to the State . . . sure of solicitude for its strength and prosperity, which the clearest dictates of self interest demand.

Obviously, to 'speak to the State', science must present itself as a good investment: that is only natural since the State dispenses tax-payers' money and must justify its expenditure. The Treasury had, of course, given special grants from time to time for special scientific work: topographical and hydrographical, sending scientists, naturalists and geologists on naval expeditions, with artists to make pictorial records. Specially remembered among such are those by *Endeavour* under Captain Cook with whom Joseph Banks sailed, *Beagle* with Darwin and *Rattlesnake* with Huxley. Moreover the Treasury funded the Royal Observatory because astronomical observation was essential for navigation and British supremacy at sea.

But the Treasury made no provision for the training of scientists. 'Laissez faire', free trade, self help, these were the maxims on which the Government was still relying around mid-century. Britain was booming and so long as things were getting on so well without Government help, why not let them be? So science had to manage with private donations and only a few Government grants for special projects. The new Owen's College at Manchester, later Manchester University, was the gift of a successful manufacturer, John Owen and up till 1914 was only getting 25 per cent of its revenue from Government grants. Leeds University was a civic foundation. Any State grant for building and minimal equipment had to be fought for. Battling for funds is time-wasting and exhausting, and the Treasury was often puzzled over which scientific investment would give best return for its money. It was largely Prince Albert's influence, and the success of the 1851 Exhibition inspired by him, that began to win some recognition for Science as important to the State and to Industry. The Treasury had got so far as to grant the Royal Society £1000 a year in 1849 and to found the Royal School of Mines in 1851. In 1853 the Department of Science and Art was set up, following the Great Exhibition, and began to help with grants for science, applied science and technical training. The Department was in continual conflict with the Treasury until the Royal Society was called in to advise on the granting of funds.

However, science and the scientist were gradually becoming professional and by the end of the century grants were becoming more readily available to Universities, to Institutions and to the rapidly increasing number of Polytechnics. By the Balfour Act of 1902 government support for secondary education was established, and this was perhaps the best 'grant' of all to science, for it provided the solid grounding on which later technical scientific training could be based. This was the ladder which in Germany had served to produce the mass of trained industrial scientists and allowed her to forge ahead while

England hesitated, causing Dewar to complain that 'German chemical industries are very largely founded upon basic discoveries made by English chemists but never properly appreciated or scientifically developed in the land of their birth'. He could have been thinking of his experience with his flask. Again it was Baeyer in Germany who developed the dye industry, based on an important discovery made in England by William Perkin of dyes from coal tar. This situation had existed for a long time; as early as 1812 Davy was writing that 'Germany still continued the great school of practical chemistry, and at this period it gained an ascendancy of no mean character over the rest of Europe.' Now, in late-20th-century Britain, so much and so many depend on grants and millions are poured out on expensive research until one wonders, could it be self defeating? Give a man a near-perfect laboratory (my brother Lawrence Bragg used to say) and he will waste his time trying to make it quite perfect. Where is the optimum?

By the turn of the century, though science was only beginning to rise to power, the scientist was enjoying his new professional status, and scientific research was now recognised as worthy a wage as well as respect. Members of the R I came to listen to scientists lecturing with a new professional confidence (however nervous they felt as they entered the theatre).

In the room outside the lecture theatre there hangs a large canvas portraying Dewar giving a lecture on 'Liquid Hydrogen Calorimetry' in 1904, and it is a pictorial record of the people who came to the R I; one can see what sort of people they were. Dewar is pouring out a boiling liquid gas and is surrounded by a galaxy of distinguished scientists and learned men, backed by tiers of ladies and gentlemen in evening dress. It is a sober and dignified contrast to Gillray's cheerful satire of the same scene a hundred years before. The Duke of Northumberland, the President, is shown in the Chair (actually it was Crichton Browne who presided that evening, but perhaps the Duke meant to come and the artist accepted the will for the deed). The representation generally may not be quite literal, but I think one can accept the audience shown as being broadly characteristic of a historic Friday Discourse.

Sitting in the front row is Lord Rayleigh, Professor of Natural Philosophy at the R I for eighteen years, an aristocratic scientist of the old school. The year the picture was painted Rayleigh and Sir William Ramsay were awarded the Nobel Prize for their joint discovery of argon.

Rayleigh had been Cavendish Professor at Cambridge, and would be President of the Royal Society; he was one of the great figures who brought balance and system into the scientific thought of his time. Also sitting in front is Sir William Crookes who discovered thallium and established the properties of cathode rays. He was Secretary of the RI and Dewar's friend until Dewar fell out with him as he did with so many people. However, they had written a paper together in 1903 and for many years made daily analyses of London's water supply, a utilitarian job in the old RI tradition. Sir William Huggins, the Astronomer Royal, is present, Lord and Lady Kelvin, the Monds, Lord Lister and Marconi; also Arthur Balfour the Prime Minister. He may have come because his sister Lady Rayleigh brought him, but he must have had a genuine interest in science for he was to be President of the British Association that summer. The Lord Chancellor (Lord Halsbury) and the Chief Justice (Lord Alverstone) have also come to listen. Fortunately there is a key to the painting and I have tried to find a profession or description for as many of the names as I could.

My list shows a proportion of 22 scientists of different kinds, 9 medical men and 12 engineers. Civil engineers would not have been considered good enough class to be admitted to membership of the RI in old days; they were lumped with landscape gardeners and most architects – the couple of electrical engineers represent a very new profession. The Law is well represented by 15 names: several judges, and barristers in plenty. One wonders if this is the influence of the great legal family, the Pollocks (Sir Frederick and Edward Pollock are both in the audience with their ladies, and Pollocks had much to do with the RI) – or indeed whether these legal people were Dewar's friends made during his frequent appearances in the Courts. There are several Members of Parliament in the audience, a few 'industrialists', an 'inventor', a well known educationalist – Sir Philip Magnus, and a couple of peers who did not claim a profession then. I have identified one musician, Sir Alexander Mackenzie, Director of the Royal Academy of Music of which Dewar was a Governor (Dewar had a passionate love of music and Sir Alexander was one of his cronies). There is a noticeable absence of the Church, though that is understandable considering what the feelings between science and religion had been during the preceding years. But why are literature and the fine arts so poorly represented on the whole? Of course there would be a preponderance of scientists at a scientific lecture, but even allowing for

that, and remembering those I could not trace and the many anony-
mous heads in the back seats, I still think that it looks as though cultures
were dividing: even though all the educated in 1904 still shared a
background of classics.

These were the intellectual élite of London, largely professional
people, very different from those who had crowded the Institution's
'green benches' a hundred years before. The hereditary peers who in
the beginning had promoted science at the R I had been the first to start
departing; then around mid century the gentlemen amateurs of wide
interests began to be replaced by members of the swelling professional
class. Through the latter part of the century these came to the R I to find
out what was going on in the intellectual world, hear of new developments in the arts and sciences, especially the sciences. The R I was still
the best place to come to for all-round interest.

The picture shows the Institution at a peak before decline; thereafter
membership began to drop slowly, then to plummet understandably in
1914. For a long time science had been growing too difficult, less
popular. Davy had been lionised by Society, Faraday could have been
so had he wished it; Tyndall dined at aristocratic tables and knew the
prominent men of his day. But after the turn of the century it was the
literary lion who held greater attention in the drawing room (or the
returned explorer or artist, but the literary man talked best). The
scientist was no longer courted as he had been. As a professional he was
too much of a specialist, and becoming very middle class. Science
became unfashionable.

Through the first decade of this century Dewar was continuing his
low temperature work, and some splendid lectures were given. Pierre
Curie gave a Discourse in 1903 and next year Rutherford's name
appears on the list for the first time with a talk on 'The Radiation and
Emanation of Radium'; next time he spoke, in 1908, his subject was
'Radio Activity'. My father W.H. Bragg gave his first Discourse with
the same title in 1911. We were proud of our Empire in that decade:
Lord Roberts talked on 'Imperial Defence' in 1906; we were stirred by
Arctic exploration, and Captain Scott spoke of 'The Forthcoming
Antarctic Expedition' in 1910; and Lord Montagu of Beaulieu talked
about 'The Modern Motor Car'.

But in spite of this excellent fare offered, people were less interested to
come to lectures than they had been; moreover with new possibilities of
grants for research and new laboratories being built, the R I laboratory

began to seem rather a one-man-band. One senses that the Institution was settling into a quiet seclusion with a core of nice middle class members interested in science who came week after week to hear a Discourse, no matter what it was about. They were still there (rather more faded) when the Braggs arrived after the First War.

The story of the RI in the 1914–18 war is rather depressing. The Secretary when war started was Alexander Siemens, the German-born industrialist. Suspicion of anybody or anything German was rife; Siemens, though naturalized British, was suspect. The Managers' Minutes record that Crichton Browne (Treasurer) was forced to allay suspicion by calling in the CID to search the RI for any 'arsenal' or other enemy equipment that might be concealed there. But the club life' of the Institution went on much the same, there is no break or change in character of the lecture lists save for the introduction of some lectures bearing on the conflict, such as one on 'La France dans l'Histoire comme Champion du Droit' and one on 'The Prevention of Trench Feet'. Sadly the laboratory which had been the pride of British science in the 19th century achieved very little, and did little to help the war effort. That is a mark of how the RI had been left behind, allowing itself to be overtaken by new developments, new ways of organising research. Dewar and the Managers were hidebound by the old tradition of private exclusiveness.

In May 1915 the War Office wrote asking if the RI would put a laboratory at their disposal for some six weeks for one of their men to test optical instruments for supply to the troops (optical glass had been imported from Germany, and in 1915 England was in difficulty). In reply to their request the WO was sent the normal form of application sent to a research worker desiring to join the Davy–Faraday Laboratory. The WO was justifiably annoyed and a certain official wrote such an 'impertinent' letter to the RI that Dewar got the President (the Duke of Northumberland) to write and complain to Lord Kitchener about it. Criticism in the Press, however, stirred the Managers to make a loyal gesture, and letters were sent to the First Lord of the Admiralty, and the Secretary of the State for War, the Minister of Munitions, and the Chairman of the Inventions Board saying, roughly speaking, 'do let us know if we can help with anything to do with chemical or physical science'. There were only three or four workers left in the DF during the war years; one would think the empty labs might have been put to more purpose.

Next year, 1916, a request came from the Ministry of Munitions for laboratory space for their staff to investigate the synthetic production of ammonium nitrate and nitric acid, and they hoped for Dewar's co-operation: but Dewar pointed out that the experiments would be dangerous, space was cramped, and anyway the investigations could not be done in time to help the war then waging. The application was withdrawn. The Naval Airship Station wrote asking if the RI would lend Dewar's air liquefying plant for experiments; Dewar wrote back that the plant was old and unreliable. The Board of Inventions and Research consulted Dewar on a subject much his own, 'the combined application of liquid air and charcoal for the production of high vacua to replace the present mercury and molecular pumps'. Again there were difficulties and some argument. To piece together a story from the Managers' Minutes is as hard as to pick up a conversation from a moving crowd, one catches a beginning or an end, rarely both. However, in the 1918 record one picks up some more cheerful ends, letters of acknowledgement of work done at the RI from half-a-dozen Government departments. Perhaps the RI had 'done its bit' after all. It is significant of the Institution's proud attitude that Dewar claimed that the various investigations done for the Government were all paid for by the RI, any inventions freely given.

But Dewar was disheartened; although his work on the absorbent power of charcoal was put to great use in the design of gas masks for the forces, his expertise and knowledge of explosives were never called for. Dewar had served on the Explosives Commission in 1888–9 and with Sir Frederick Abel had invented cordite, although it had involved a long lawsuit with the Swedish firm of Nobel to prove it was an English invention.

Disappointed, and unable to continue his low temperature work because of the expense in war time, Dewar reverted to an old love, his interest in thin films; soap bubbles had been the subject of his first set of Juvenile lectures at Christmas 1877. Now he made flat films and studied them with Newton's interference colours; he made 'black' films, colour-less because only a few molecules thick. He blew long-lasting soap bubbles, blew them inside huge bottles and cherished them for months. Enjoyment he may have had with his bubbles and films, but the old fighter meant to make the most out of them too: in 1915 he was applying for patent rights for 'Improvement in means for obtaining liquid films and observing light effects thereon and the utilization thereof for various purposes . . .' There was opposition, and two years later he is writing that 'litigation had been started in the Courts with regard to my patent rights'. Dewar was so often fighting and arguing; perhaps he did so much as an expert witness not only to make money but also because he enjoyed the atmosphere of a Court.

He was essentially an artist in his experimenting and in his lecture presentation; he was a musician, playing his fiddle far into the night, accompanied by his wife; he wrote charming comic verse for the 'Bee Club' (a club for convivial young chemists); and he loved beautiful things of fine craftsmanship, and collected them. There is charm in the very titles he chose for his Christmas lectures – 'Clouds and Cloudland', 'Frost and Fire', 'A Soap Bubble', 'Alchemy' – and a story-tale quality about the old man of eighty climbing up to the attics of the RI to measure the sky radiation, night after night, with his charcoal gas thermoscope – while the RI below him slept, literally and figuratively, and the Davy–Faraday Laboratory slept even more soundly. On 23 March 1923 James Dewar himself sank to his last sleep.

SIX

The Change in Outlook

W.H. BRAGG, H. DALE, E. RIDEAL, E. ANDRADE, W.L. BRAGG

DEWAR'S REIGN had been long with no great landmarks of change. It was the world outside which was changing, while after the turn of the century the pace of the Institution was slowing down, in spite of the new opportunities available in the DF laboratories. This recession was reflected in the RI membership, which dropped every year from 1905 to 1917.

Dewar was the last of the line of great scientists who came to the RI as young men (he was the oldest of them, thirty-five) and made their finest discoveries there. Since his time, Directors have been appointed for eminence already achieved elsewhere. Dewar was the lone researcher like his predecessors in the laboratory, and under him the RI kept much of its private 'Lit. and Phil.' character. When he went it was the end of an era. I saw that end myself, for Dewar's successor as 'Fullerian Professor of Chemistry, Superintendent of the House, and Director of the Davy–Faraday Laboratory' was my father, William Henry Bragg, and in 1923 we came to live at the RI.

My father asked himself, and from that time on Resident Professors have asked themselves: 'What can I do with this beautiful old place; what part can the RI play in the twentieth century?' Each Resident Professor has made his special contribution to the answer, and now in the 1980s the RI is thriving and much alive. This chapter tells of the earlier stages in the new development, and I think it is worth beginning by trying to make some picture of what the Institution was like in 1923 at that pause before the turning of the tide. For the tide did turn then. Looking back I think anyone must see that it was WHB (as I will call my father) who brought new life and started the RI on a new course; though one must remember that change was waiting in the wings, that the RI must have changed then anyway to go on living in the new post-war world. We must remember too the difference the War had made to the outlook on science and the organization of scientific research. WHB came to Albemarle Street at just the moment to usher in that change at the RI, and under his direction the Davy–Faraday Laboratory sprang to life, and was steered into new ways.

First I would like to describe a very superficial view of the Institution at its lowest ebb, of how it appeared to a girl of sixteen who looked at everything and everybody with excited curiosity; how it looked to me. I think the principal impression was one of beauty and rather shabby dignity, of dust and age, of quiet. The core of the social, the 'club' life of the Institution has been the 'Discourse' on Friday evenings ever since Faraday instituted these in 1826. On these evenings I encountered the Members gathered in the Library before the lecture. The Managers stood grouped near the blazing fire dressed in white ties and tails, ready to welcome people arriving, their ladies in evening dresses that I soon came to know well, and long white gloves. Sir James Crichton Browne would be at the centre. He had been Treasurer since 1889 and had done much to keep the RI going in Dewar's latter years. It was he who had presented the Managers' invitation to my father to come to the RI, calling on him in person at University College, dressed in frock coat and top hat. He was over eighty, very deaf, and wore dundreary whiskers that descended in a straggle from cheek bones to collar. He had been a famous 'alienist', what we now call a mental specialist. The Secretary was charming Sir Arthur Keith, anthropologist and a Scot; he was a great supporter, and he and his wife became Bragg family friends. Then there was the old Norfolk squire Sir Lawrence Jones, scion of the agricultural landlord tradition, and dear Lady Jones, who meant to take notes in lectures with her golden fountain pen, but who usually went to sleep and snored.

There were so many Members to get to know, distinguished, stuffy, kind to the newcomers, and welcoming; I can only tell of a few. Sir James Frazer (of *The Golden Bough*) sometimes came, shuffling in after his militant wife who advanced with ear trumpet thrust before her to catch greetings. And the Dowager Lady Winchilsea was sometimes there; I pick her out because she links back through RI history, for the first President of the RI was the 9th Earl of Winchilsea, and she herself came of the Harcourt family. A Harcourt had launched the British Association at York in 1831, and the family kept up a private laboratory. Lady Winchilsea employed a stenographer to take down scientific lectures, and kept a scrap of Mme Curie's radium in her linen cupboard, so her grand-daughter has told me. Then there was Mr Stone, the old Edwardian beau with waxed moustache and pearl tie-pin who had been coming to the R I since the days when it had still been rather fashionable to come. The Rayleighs came, and Sir Oliver Lodge, and Miss Willmott of gardening fame; and Major Phillips, gentleman dilettante who painted and played the fiddle, who also had his own laboratory. And of course there was old Miss This and old Miss That; they all seemed so old to me when I was sixteen, except for those few daughters brought for culture, as Lady Palmerston had brought hers a century before, or as Louisa Hamilton, Tyndall's bride, had been brought. Everybody was very kind, but most of them rather stiff with age.

The adjective 'old' comes again and again – old Halford, the head porter, old Heath the lecture assistant who had lost an eye in one of Dewar's experiments, and nervous old Henry Young the assistant secretary, a Sandemanian who had known Faraday and who had been so frightened of Dewar. He would have no telephone or typewriter in his office off the front hall. In those days you entered from the street straight into the front hall to mount the dividing staircase to the Library, nearly always empty save for a white bearded old gentleman who sat day after day in the same chair reading and making notes in the margin of his book (the Librarian said he didn't like rubbing them out because they were so interesting). But if instead of going up from the hall you went down to the basement (past the Model Room which housed Tyndall's and Faraday's and Davy's old apparatus and the remnant of Rumford's model collection), you found Dewar's huge old engines for liquefying gases and a general air of dim desolation smelling of old chemicals, the only live thing an enormous heating furnace. As for the Davy–Faraday Laboratory, it too was almost deserted; there was only one regular worker left in its many rooms.

I must move on, and from this page onwards I shall make a change in the manner of telling this story about the R I, its people, activities and contacts with the world outside. The scale and tempo must quicken as we near the present day. For one reason, the Resident Professors were for many years of my own family, my father from 1923–42 and my brother from 1953–66, and I have already written in my biography of my father at some length about his time at the R I, with many references to my brother. Up to now I have allotted one chapter to each Resident Professor, but in this there will be five professors; I move more swiftly over their lives because it takes time for events and trends to settle to a readable pattern, and the nearer one gets to the present the harder it is to assess developments still in active growth in living hands. This said, I return to 1923, to write about my father's arrival at the Institution, sketching briefly something of his life before he came there.

WHB was born in 1862, a farmer's son in a remote corner of west Cumberland, who trudged across the fields to the village school, and then on the death of his mother was snatched away, aged seven, by a benevolently imperious uncle, to be educated in Market Harborough where the uncle had been instrumental in reviving the old grammar school which had lapsed. Through scholarships WHB reached Cambridge and read mathematics at Trinity College in the true Cambridge tradition for a scientist in the 1880s; and at the age of twenty-three sailed to Australia to take up the appointment of Professor of Mathematics and Physics at the University of colonial Adelaide. He learned physics on the boat. He spent over twenty years teaching at Adelaide, and himself wrote that he never thought of doing research until he was over forty. Then, questioning some of Madame Curie's findings (the scientific world was very excited about the Curies' work on radium) he experimented and found what turned out to be the right interpretation, which fitted in with the radio-active work that Rutherford had been doing at McGill University in Montreal. He wrote to Rutherford; and had to wait three months for the answer to reach him. Rutherford pronounced his interpretation to be right, and that was the start of his life's research and of a long friendship with Rutherford. Recognition brought WHB back to England to a professorship at Leeds in 1909 with the family he had acquired by then. He had married Gwendoline, daughter of Sir Charles Todd, the grand old man who had laid the Overland Telegraph line across the unexplored centre of Australia. It was Faraday's friend Airy who had sent Todd out from Greenwich to be Astronomer at Adelaide. In 1915 WHB resigned from Leeds to come to University College, London. He was away on war work for the Admiralty from 1916 to 1918, then back to UCL, whence he came to the RI.

WHB's research at UCL had been on X-rays and crystal analysis and he had gathered a team of research workers. There would be plenty of room for his team in the empty DF. Although Dewar had been Director of the Davy–Faraday since Scott left, he had continued to carry on his own research in the RI basement. The new conception in 1923 was to use the Davy–Faraday Laboratory for the RI professor's own research: to establish a research school attached to the RI and to amalgamate the interests of the RI and DF.

Team work in the laboratory is essentially a 20th-century development; now teams (especially American ones) have often swelled to a prodigious size. A team could scarcely have been possible at the RI in the last century for lack of space and lack of money. It was only possible in 1923 because the Davy–Faraday was practically empty (Dewar having cannily let it run down in latter years, to free it for his successor, as Mr Green his assistant once explained to me) and also because WHB had support for his team with a government grant from the Department of Scientific and Industrial Research. For a grant to come to the RI (for we can think of the DF's and the RI's interests as being amalgamated henceforward) was also a revolution in the life of the Institution which had been so private and independent of outside influence and support. Dewar had been wary of such help. In his Presidential Address to the British Association in 1902 he said:

The installations required by the refinements of modern science are continually becoming more costly, so that upon all grounds it would appear that without endowments . . . the outlook for disinterested research is rather dark. On the other hand these endowments, unless carefully administered, might obviously tend to impair the single-minded devotion to the search after truth for its own sake, to which science has owed every memorable advance made in the past.

Certainly this was the way that science had advanced at the RI, and Dewar stuck to the tradition. But the DSIR grant was a grant without ties and in that sense the Davy-Faraday did keep its independence.

The Bragg name is associated with X-ray crystallography whose story starts in 1912 and introduces my brother. Since I never called him Lawrence myself I shall refer to him here as WL.

In 1912 von Laue in Germany published some results on X-ray diffraction by crystals which bore on the research work on X-rays that WHB had been doing at Leeds. WHB sensed a puzzle in Laue's results and called his son's attention to the problem (WL was working in the Cavendish Laboratory). WL in an intuitive flash conceived an explanation; his father recognised it as the answer and with brilliantly swift expertise designed his famous spectrometer, so bringing WL's idea to fruit. There is a moment when an idea hovers for someone to catch: without WHB, WL's idea might have continued as speculation until some other worker in the field had solved the problem and published first. Working excitedly together at Leeds in 1912–13, they began to solve the problems of crystal structure as though X-rays had given them eyes to see and means to plot the arrangements of atoms within the molecules: a matter of importance to chemists as well as physicists. It was W L alone who worked out the structure of common salt, whereas they jointly solved that of diamonds; these two substances being prototypes of the inorganic and the organic worlds which they and their pupils were to explore so extensively in the years to follow. I remember my father handling the models with a look of inner happiness, holding up the model in a beam of light to throw its shadow on the screen and turning it to show the arrangement of atoms in different planes. There were always little balls and bits of models lying about in my father's study in my childhood; in his pen tray a small 'carbon ring' – black, with amber and green balls that took on and off. Salt and diamond – these were only the beginnings of the story of X-ray crystallography which has revealed the atomic structure of the natural world, from the simplest salts to the macromolecules in living cells. War in 1914 stopped co-operation of father and son completely, but they had opened up a whole new field of investigation, the huge subject of X-ray crystallography.

It was at Leeds that a haze of misunderstanding began to gather over and between father and son about recognition of their respective shares in the joint initial discovery. The shadow of this haze lasted until after my father's death, but it never broke the ties in a closely knit family. Father and son never managed to discuss their scientific relationships thoroughly, WHB being very reserved and WL inclined to bottle up his feelings. But warm if somewhat anxious affection flowed from father to son always and, though from son to father the affection was sometimes hurt, it was always warmed by great respect. WL never failed to consult his father about the prospects of any new job that was offered to him.

The team which my father WHB gathered after the war, starting at University College London and developing further in the Davy–Faraday Laboratory after 1923, included Dame Kathleen Lonsdale (Miss Yardley at that time), J.D. Bernal, J.M. Robertson (later Professor at Glasgow), W.T. Astbury (who went to Leeds) and A. Müller. They worked for minimal salaries (paid out of the grant), but they had an exciting time in the twenties and thirties on early X-ray and crystal work. Many applied to join the DF team for a while, some coming on grants from their own universities or other scientific bodies. After a spell at the DF they often went out as disciples to promote the new work in other centres. Writing about the scientific side Astbury explained that WHB 'was not an active participant in everything, naturally, nor the originator of every new idea, but he was the soul of everything.' Rutherford as visiting professor at the RI was also often in the laboratory. WHB was so gentle and quiet; Rutherford so richly boisterous, encouraging and exuberant, making the team all laugh with his stories. Nor did they need much encouragement to enjoy themselves. A room at the top of the DF was set aside for table tennis and they all grew so expert that extra rules had to be invented to make the game more difficult, like having to hit small blocks of wood off the table. The annual tournament was a great event.

Not only the Davy–Faraday Laboratory, but also the Institution itself began to wake to fresh life. The rather narrow atmosphere of the old 'Lit. and Phil.' club was enriched by drawing in new people from outside the RI. My parents gave dinner parties before the Friday Discourses and received, most warmly, in the flat after each lecture. My mother was a good hostess and loved making a party 'go'. Of course it was no kind of 'salon' that she made (she had the wit but lacked the knowledge); but she made friends, and people near her made friends with each other. She did much for the RI with her energy and warmth. They were what the RI needed at that time.

After my mother's death in 1929 I had to take on the woman's job at the RI and play hostess for my father. I was twenty-two and very frightened. We continued my mother's tradition of inviting the lecturer and his wife to dine on Friday nights, and asking guests to meet them. This made new friends for the Institution. We would sit down ten for dinner. Now, as hostess I felt very grand, very anxious. There were some awful moments. Once H.G. Wells was the lecturer, sitting on my right – and talking nervously I flipped my glass of claret which spurted over his white shirt front. In agony I rushed him to the bathroom and mopped; but it was no good. We telephoned to his house and the parlour maid dashed with a clean shirt in a taxi. He did not get over it; the lecture was fine, but after, though it looked as if I were trying to monopolise him, really he was muttering, 'I don't want to be introduced to *anybody*', while the dowagers stood around looking at me over his shoulder.

Twice it happened that guests muddled the Fridays and arrived on the wrong one. The first time there was astonishment and a confusion of apologies. The following week again extra guests were announced; but we never let on – my father gave me a quiet wink and I slipped out to get extra places laid at table, and our guests never found out till they said to each other as they were returning home, 'I thought we were going to Mr Snook's lecture, not Sir Somebody Something's' – and looked up the invitation. That mistake was made by a subsequent Director, E.N. da C. Andrade. He made other mistakes, but he was always a loyal admirer of my parents.

In 1932 I was married. But marriage did not take us away for long; a beloved aunt came over from Australia to look after my father for 18 months; and then my husband and I came back again. Our children were the first ever to live in the Royal Institution. We kept the pram with the historic apparatus in what then remained of Rumford's Model Room, beside the lift.

Soon after there was another upheaval, when in 1935 the Libraries were rebuilt, also the dining room and drawing room of the flat. Again there was moving and mess and money raising. The result, the rooms of the Library as you now see them.

Interestingly, the utilitarian aims of the RI were revived – not directly, but through my father's work for the DSIR. Tirelessly he worked to get science to the help of industry in that low time of the twenties, and visited countless factories to encourage new industrial research. We have almost forgotten how reluctant industry was to accept science then. The very success of British industry in the 19th century had bred among manufacturers a complacency about their products that disinclined them to spend money on research or to alter their ways. It had been a different climate a century earlier, when industrialists had courted applied science. But the Faraday Centenary Exhibition in 1931 showed what had been done, with its mighty display of new industries sprung from scientific discovery. For a week in the Albert Hall the electric, electromagnetic and all the industries derived from Faraday's electrical work exhibited their latest developments, radiating from the small simple pieces of apparatus in the centre of the Hall that Faraday had made and used himself. These were insignificant looking and shabby, so to show their importance was one of the problems facing the designers of the exhibition. To live without electric light, telephone, radio, refrigeration (the list can go on and on) is almost unthinkable now: Faraday's scientific investigations have benefited mankind as Rumford meant that investigations at the RI should do, but not at all in Rumford's way. The Count saw investigation aimed at a direct end: Faraday's discoveries were made with no end in view save to establish new truth. As my brother put it, the way of advance is for pure science to feed a reservoir of knowledge, from which technology will draw, perhaps years later.

The RI aim of 'diffusion of knowledge' was given a new opening between the wars. Sound broadcasting was a new way to get science across, and WHB gained a reputation for popular science talks on what was then called the 'wireless'. But when the BBC decided that science should be relegated to the 'schools programme' WHB resigned, disappointed that the importance for everybody of a basic general knowledge of science and the scientist's point of view was not yet recognised. Science, though rising to power, was still receiving snubs.

WHB, the most modest and gentle of men, pursued relentlessly his vision of what science must try to do for industry and education, and in national affairs also. His main reason for leaving Leeds and coming to London in 1915 had been his anxiety to use any influence he had to get science to help the country, not only in the War, but in the difficult times ahead that any thinking person could foresee. He was on the Council of the Royal Society and he felt, 'The Royal ought to have its eye on all the possibilities of encouraging scientific application, should know what is to be done, be in touch with universities and research laboratories, be ready to advise and co-ordinate . . .'

When the Second World War came he was at the RI and also President of the Royal Society, and in 1940 he wrote as PRS to the Prime Minister Winston Churchill to urge the setting up of a committee to advise the Government on scientific matters. Somewhat grudgingly the Scientific Advisory Committee was formed under Lord Hankey's chairmanship. The Committee did do useful work, and it was even asked to report on the Atom Bomb: but Churchill preferred more individualistic and secret ways of coming to decisions (the Bomb had been practically decided on before the Committee was asked to advise). However, science had gradually been winning a place in the Establishment as was shown by the setting up of the Medical Research Council in 1920 and the Agricultural Research Council in 1931. After the end of the 1930s the DSIR no longer needed to battle to get science used, and money was beginning to pour into industrial research. There the battle had been won in that generation.

In the early days of the Second World War my father said to me, 'I shan't live to see the end of this', and he did not; he died in 1942. Sir Henry Dale (who had succeeded WHB as President of the Royal Society in 1940) now took over at the RI as a 'caretaker' job for the rest of the war. He was a great pharmacologist and physiologist who had the same quiet kindness as my father. Before the First World War he had been Director of the Wellcome Research Laboratories for about nine years, moving in 1914 to what became in 1920 the National Institute for Medical Research, and of this too he was Director from 1928 until he retired in 1942.

When the war was over, Sir Henry retired also from the RI, and the Managers appointed Eric Rideal, later Sir Eric, as Resident Professor. Once again, after five years of war, new life had to be breathed into the RI. There was much to do to assess the outlook of people and the needs of science in the tired and hungry confusion of post-war Britain: and there was financial stringency of course. However, the Friday discourses and the Christmas lectures, those hardy perennials, had survived to bloom vigorously again with children back from evacuation in the country and nights freed from the menace of air raids. The Davy–Faraday Laboratory had lost most of its workers to war jobs, but life had been maintained there with some women researchers and refugee scientists. Rideal soon filled up the laboratory with young research workers to carry on the colloid chemistry investigations he had been doing in Cambridge, and got grants from Government and Industry for re-equipping the laboratory. Not especially interested in experimenting with his own hands, he had a gift for inspiring the better students; it is recorded that forty-seven of his students went on to be professors. Rideal had a very human ideal for science; he was interested in his students as people, interested in Christian Socialism, and in the assistance that applied science could give to the nation. He had a strong sense of humour, yet hid his heart under a somewhat crabbed manner. But the 'club' side of the RI was too much for the Rideals, especially for charming and sensitive Lady Rideal, struggling to entertain in those difficult years of shortages – more difficult than the war years themselves. Sir Eric proposed that leadership be divided, that he should carry on as Director of the Davy–Faraday and that a new professor be appointed to take charge of the Institution's affairs. The Managers could not agree to this, the President, Lord Brabazon, declaring that 'there cannot be two kings in Babylon.' So Rideal resigned. E.N. da C. Andrade, Professor at University College London and Vice President of the RI, let it be known that he would like to succeed Rideal; and he was appointed. Andrade had the RI under his hand at last, as he had long wanted to have it. It was not to be a gentle hand.

The Managers might have known better; my brother WL told me that Andrade was ever a stormy petrel (he had known him on war service in France). On the face of it Andrade had just the qualifications for the RI professorship: not only was he a brilliant physicist (his principal work the flow of liquids and solids) but he was also a poet (better than Davy) and friend of poets, an authority on the history of science, and a collector of old scientific books. In addition he was a reformer, an aggressive reformer, and once at the RI he set out to make his presence felt.

The basic trouble was the continuing 'club' character of the Institution, inherited from its beginnings when the President and the Managers had represented the owning Proprietors. The altered Constitution of 1810 had substituted Members for Proprietors, but the Managers had continued to function in the old way, firmly holding the reins. Andrade had expected that his high-sounding titles – Fullerian Professor of Chemistry, Superintendent of the House, and Director of the Davy–Faraday Laboratory – would give him the position of Managing Director of the Institution; but the President, Brabazon, maintained that a club could not have a 'Director', that Andrade only had that courtesy title in the RI as Director of the DF Laboratory. Andrade was bent on altering things; there was friction over who held the power. My father WHB used to say that the Constitution of the RI only ran on good-will; there was so much of it when he was around. Under Andrade's aggressive zeal the RI groaned in pain and ground almost to a halt. In March 1952 Andrade lost a vote of confidence from the Members and resigned. Arbitration over his claim for compensation for being turned out was not settled until a year later when the RI had to pay him a large sum. In April 1953 the Managers offered my brother Sir (William) Lawrence Bragg the vacant professorship: with much hesitation he accepted.

My brother WL was born in 1890 in Australia and, aged 18, already graduated with an Honours degree in Natural Science from Adelaide University, returned to England with the family in 1909. He went up to Trinity College Cambridge and took a First in the Natural Science

Tripos, staying on to work in the Cavendish Laboratory. There he made that initial break-through in research which started the subject of X-ray and crystal analysis. Father and son were awarded a joint Nobel Prize in 1915. WL was only 25; he got the news when he was with the army in France and the village curé on whom he was billeted behind the lines brought up a bottle of wine from his cellar to celebrate. WL spent his wartime in developing a system of Sound Ranging, a method of locating enemy guns by the sound of their firing. His father was doing more or less parallel work, locating enemy submarines by echo sounding for the Admiralty.

After the Armistice my brother was appointed Professor of Physics at Manchester, succeeding Rutherford who had gone to the Cavendish. At first WL had a tough time at Manchester. He was an inexperienced lecturer then, and students were rowdy; but he collected a team of research workers and the X-ray and crystal work began to blossom. In 1937 he moved to the National Physical Laboratory, encouraged by his father who ever had the interests of science in industry at heart. WL was delighted to move his wife from grimy Manchester to Bushy House at Teddington, the beautiful Georgian mansion where William IV and Queen Adelaide had lived. But less than a year later WL was invited to the Cavendish after Rutherford's sudden death. To be Cavendish Professor at Cambridge is the most desirable position in England for any physicist, and WL accepted; his wife left Bushy House with great regret, before even the new decorations had lost their pristine freshness. So WL succeeded Rutherford once again. It was not easy, either time, to succeed a man of such forceful stature and exuberant personality.

The Cavendish Laboratory had been dominated by Rutherford and his research group on nuclear physics and the atom. WL's contribution to the Cavendish was to democratise it – for he believed that 'the ideal research unit is one of six to twelve scientists with a few assistants'. But the shadow of war was already looming by the time WL took on the Cavendish, and for the next years he became pre-occupied with the scientific needs of the country at war, and with sorting out the right scientists to help in the right places. In 1941 he was in America as senior liaison officer with American and Canadian scientists, and in 1943 he had himself flown to neutral Sweden. Yet during that first year at Cambridge he had discovered Max Perutz in the crystallography laboratory – or rather Perutz had found him and shown him his X-ray photograph of haemoglobin: WL had immediately realised the thrilling possibility of extending crystal analysis to the structure of the living cell. This was to become the main thread of his research for the rest of his life.

In 1952 the Andrade trouble at the RI blew up. WL had been watching the storm gathering and had tried to help; he had been a visiting professor since 1938. Then came the invitation to take over at the RI in Andrade's place. WL debated – it would not be too strong to say agonised. If succeeding Rutherford twice had been hard, succeeding Andrade was harder. Ought he, or ought he not, to go to the RI?

The Managers at the Institution had turned out a man who was a scientist of repute, who had been an admirer of my father WHB, and was a friend of the Bragg family. Many in the scientific world, especially at the Royal Society, thought that Andrade had been turned out unfairly. The conventions of professional etiquette at the least were against accepting the job in such a situation; but WL was not a conventional person, and he also understood the dire predicament of the Royal Institution. If no scientist felt he could decently go there after what had happened, the RI would die (and some, I believe, thought that that would be the best thing). Lecturing at the RI as a visiting professor, WL had felt anxiously involved in its troubles, and he had a family loyalty to the Institution. Choosing between a point of professional honour and the RI, he chose the RI. He suffered for it; criticism closed doors to him for the next few years, and even friends were doubtful. But in the outcome he lived down criticism to win admiration instead, and, with strong support from his wife Alice, gave new life to the RI after completing the sore job of nursing it back to normality. Through those early bad years he also had the satisfying reward of being able to continue the protein research programme which, like a plant divided, flourished abundantly in the Davy–Faraday as well as in the Cavendish.

The administrative problem remained unsolved at Andrade's departure, but persuasion, patience and an anxiety on everyone's part to restore the dignity of the Institution at length resolved the old difficulty. During discussions aimed at finding WL's successor it was agreed that Sir George Porter should in due course be appointed as 'Director of the Royal Institution', and in 1965 this title was formally bestowed upon WL himself. Thus was the way prepared.

When newly arrived in 1953 WL had to face innumerable questions. Finance was a crucial one: Andrade had spent much of the Institution's dwindling resources and had had to be bought out. Members' subscriptions were quite inadequate for maintenance. And, apart from the DF laboratory, what was the RI to be maintained for anyway? What would be its function in the 1950s? The beautiful old rooms were little used save on Friday Discourse nights; quiet reigned save when children trooped in for Christmas lectures. And then the idea occurred: why should children come to lectures only at Christmas? Why should not schoolchildren come to lectures through the year? So, in 1954, the Schools Lectures were started; the RI found a new vocation as repertory theatre for school science with all the experimental expertise and resources of the RI poured into the demonstrations. The Institution's original aim of diffusion of knowledge had sprung to life again and indeed continues to put out shoots in new directions. It is so exciting and such an important conception that I shall tell about these lectures at some length in Chapters 7 and 8. But they had to be paid for.

WL went to Industry cap in hand: by this time Industry respected science as a good investment and felt some gratitude to science and scientists. He got the support needed for the lectures. He also got the support he wanted for research in the DF laboratory. He had no doubts about what he wanted to do there, but money for equipment and salaries for workers had to be found. For lectures and research (though not for general activities in the Institution itself) he was given grants by the Government, by Research Councils, as well as by Industry and Commerce. A new scheme for Corporate Subscribers was evolved whereby industrial companies gave annual contributions and in return could send a specified number of their people to enjoy lectures and all the RI had to offer. Income from these Corporate Subscribers soon amounted to more than the Members subscribed.

With my brother at the RI, the Davy–Faraday Laboratory became once again one of the principal centres for X-ray analysis. In the early days of the work it would have seemed beyond the wildest dreams to solve the complicated structures of protein molecules, but that became the main objective in the DF in the second half of the fifties under WL, working in close collaboration with Max Perutz and John Kendrew in Cambridge. Experimenting itself had been changing from a manipulative art inspired by intuitive guesswork to the assembling of a vast body of observations with a computer to sort them out, answer intelligent questions, and cope with all those calculations which filled page after page of my father's laboratory note books – not that my father or my brother sought to explain their findings in the language of mathematics, any more than Faraday had done; their approach was tangible rather than abstract.

A scientist usually has his great ideas early. Certainly my brother WL had his great idea at 22, whereas WHB had not come to research until middle age. By the time that WL was at the RI he was no longer pioneering in research himself, but was directing and counselling a team: he was in practice as well as in name the Director of the Davy–Faraday. He was a wise head of his team who had learned understanding in those fascinating but not always easy days of collaborating with an already well-known father. He knew how none must trespass, how each must feel safe to develop his own idea, either alone or with a group, until it is ready to be given to the world.

But WL's influence spread beyond the Davy–Faraday; he came to be looked up to as the father (and if so WHB was the grandfather) of an ever widening subject; its co-ordinator and inspirer. When Nobel Prizes were awarded to Perutz and Kendrew for their work on proteins, and to Crick and Watson for their analysis of DNA, his delight was unbounded. Very ill in hospital when the news reached him, he is said to have spent the night explaining the structure of DNA to his night nurse. Watson's book, *The Double Helix*, the story of the daily working out of DNA was a best seller; WL had recognised its Pepysian quality, and was instrumental in getting it published in a somewhat calmed and pruned form, himself writing a generous foreword. 'You don't know what it was like before I got at it,' WL said to me.

With the Davy–Faraday Laboratory housing a team working on the Director's line of research, there must be a problem when the Director retires; but WL negotiated a transfer of the main body of the crystallographic work and workers to Oxford, where a new Laboratory of Molecular Biophysics was created. Perutz was then head of the Molecular Biology Unit of the Medical Research Council at Cambridge. It is interesting how the X-ray crystallography work has put out shoots into other subjects, forming fresh links between disciplines which had separated out in the 19th century from the old Natural Philosophy.

Though my brother retired from being Director of the Royal Institution in 1966, he did not lose touch; he was made Professor Emeritus and went on lecturing from time to time, giving his last Schools Lecture in 1971, the year before he died. What was his contribution to the RI? If brilliance be accepted, it is character which colours what a man does. It is the personalities of these scientists at the RI which have made the

pattern – Davy's flash and dash, Faraday's patient confidence in his
search for the truths in a Universe his God had made. What of the two
Braggs in the 20-century line of succession? It is as 'the Braggs' that
they will be remembered: as well as sharing the inception of a whole new
area of research, they shared an outlook on living, and strove to impart
their sense of wonder to all men so far as men would receive it. Each
became master of the art of 'popular lecturing' and used it. The
unimaginative scholar may look down on that art – but how else to show
wonder to the common man, woman, or child? How else make them
realise their inheritance? They were wise and shrewd, those Braggs,
over great things; but at the same time delightfully unsophisticated, so
they seemed to by-pass cleverness. My father had a profound humility;
he was kind and courteous, expecting everyone to want the best, as he
did; and they usually responded. He was gentle, but he could be bold.
My brother in one respect was very different; he had the artistic
temperament of his mother and could feel passionately. I once heard a
lecturer praise the wise moderation of his letters, while W L's daughter
beside me in the audience whispered, 'that's because he always tore up
the first one!' He was an artist: he drew with brush and pencil, but also
in words; he would explain an obscure scientific point with a vivid
visual analogy – almost a poetic spotlight on the difficulty. He had the
artist's intuition to see a great idea and express it – but in doing so the
periphery must be a little out of focus and the detail round the edge
must not detract from the centre of interest. So he brooded on ideas and
observed things, but occasionally did not notice the question hovering
on the lips of the person in front of him; sometimes, if you were urgently
seeking his opinion, you noticed suddenly that his finger was in a book
or his eyes on a bird outside the window. This could make for difficulties
in committee work (which he disliked). At the Cavendish he managed
to install a second-in-command who, at a meeting, would lean forward
and say, 'We think, don't we, Professor?' But he was always shrewd
when he really grasped someone's problems. As he grew older, perhaps
less driven by fierce creative urge, he found it easier to listen and people
loved and valued his hard-won wisdom. Above all WL was never
distant with children: he loved being with them, explaining things to
them; 'We enjoy the same things,' he said. I believe most children and
great scientists enjoy the same curiosity about the natural world. I was
once walking with WL down a road where some workmen were
excavating. He crossed to peer down – then turned to me and said very

seriously, 'You should always look into a hole', and a passer-by doubled up with laughter. So when WL lectured to children he was not so much talking at them as sharing interests with them; and this created the inspiration and vitality of his Schools Lectures. I shall tell in Chapter 7 about the technique of the performance.

I think this opening of young eyes to see and ears to hear was probably his greatest contribution to the RI: its old aim brought to life in a new guise. Of course I am a sister and partial, but it is very clear that his time at the Institution served it in good stead. For the second time a Bragg brought back new life; WL brought back warmth and good humour, solved many problems, and wisely laid the scene for his eminent successor.

MARTIN AND LUCY CAROE WITH THEIR GRANDFATHER BRAGG

SEVEN

Lectures and Lecturing

NOW I HAVE brought the RI through its first 170 years I will leave it in the hands of my brother's successor, Sir George Porter – leave it to him to be making a further instalment of the story through the present day. I will only say that, as I write this page in the early 1980s, the RI is spinning like a humming top on a rising note of success. I want now to turn back again and, having told of experiments and professors, dwell instead on two aspects and aims of the Institution during the same span of years. In this chapter I shall focus on the lecture theatre, on some of the lectures given in it and the men who gave them; and how the art of lecturing was brought to such a pitch in Webster's almost perfect theatre.

Lecturing is an old art, the oldest form of teaching, and the only one when there were no printed books and few could read. In the Schools of Paris in Abelard's time, the Master first had to read aloud to his students some work of philosophy or the Early Fathers before he could expound or discuss it with them. The spread of printing in the 16th century altered lecturing; with several copies of a book available there was less need for a lecturer to read the text from his manuscript copy before discoursing on it. It is the sermon in church today which keeps the trace of a lecture in its old form: the text read out, now only a sentence or a verse from the Scriptures, followed by lessons to be drawn from it. In the 17th century the low-church parishes in East Anglia actually employed a 'lecturer': a list of 'lecturers' and rectors serving alongside each other is preserved in Dedham Church, in Essex.

One thinks of lecturing as the special province of the Universities. The more formal lecture has always been preferred in France, and in Scotland following France: the English have been inclined to favour the tutorial system and the seminar. But in the second half of the 18th century lecturing became popular throughout the country and itinerant lecturers toured. The Enlightenment in France had made intellectual pursuits fashionable; science was the new thing. In *Humphrey Clinker*, published in 1770, Smollett makes his hero Matthew Bramble say, speaking of the British Museum (open to the public in Montagu House since 1753), 'I could also wish, for the honour of the nation, that there was a complete apparatus for a course of mathematics, mechanics and experimental philosophy, and a good salary settled upon an able professor who should give popular lectures on these subjects.' The Duchess of Devonshire herself went to chemistry classes in the mornings and became a subscriber to the Royal Institution. Sir Henry Holland, later President of the RI, learnt his science from an itinerant lecturer.

When the plan to instruct artisans in simple science at the RI proved abortive, the Managers concentrated on trying to please their fashionable audience. It fell on Dr Garnett, the first professor, to think out a scheme for lectures, and he put this proposition to the Managers.

Our object ought undoubtedly to be both amusement and instruction. We shall have two classes of auditors, the one consisting of those who will come chiefly for amusement or because it may be fashionable. These it will be our business to amuse, while at the same time I hope we shall be able to interest them in the subjects, and communicate considerable knowledge without any trouble to themselves . . . each lecture to continue only an hour, that the attention may not be fatigued. For the second class of auditors – I mean those attached to scientific pursuits, I would propose a full scientific course of experimental philosophy on the plan generally adopted in Universities.

It was a hopeful plan, but had little success in practice since Garnett became worn out trying to give all the lectures himself, and departed. Thomas Young had no lecturing success either. A tutor at Emmanuel College Cambridge wrote of him: 'Young . . . was worse calculated than any man I ever knew for the communication of knowledge. I remember him taking me with him to the RI to hear him lecture to a number of silly women and dilettante philosophers. But nothing could show his judgement less than the methods he adopted; for he presumed, like many other lecturers and preachers, on the knowledge, and not the ignorance, of his hearers.' A shrewd comment.

Rumford never lectured – except over the dinner table. At the close of the century the lecturer was still just a teacher; the great Rumford could have no time for that. Even half a century later attitudes had changed and he would certainly have lectured as the expert on new developments in kitchen equiment or on his latest theories about the nature of heat: one can easily imagine Rumford giving a Friday Discourse.

It was Davy who attracted the crowd, his charm behind the lecture table that helped to pull the RI out of the worst trough in its history. Admittedly he had a flair for lecturing, but his periods were practised; he once wrote to beg Coleridge 'to come and renew his stock of metaphors'. And when the famous Dalton made the long journey by road from Manchester to give some lectures, Davy coached him carefully. Dalton had written to ask, 'Pray what is the usual duration of a lecture, one or two hours?' In a letter written after his safe return home, he explained that he 'went in a great measure unprepared, not knowing the nature and manner of the lectures at the Institution'. But Davy looked after him and he lodged in the RI. Dalton gave twenty lectures, stayed six weeks and went home happy; he had found his audience '*learned* and *attentive*, though many of them of rank', and his lectures 'were received with the greatest applause'.

From the moment he came to the RI in 1813 Faraday studied scrupulously the art of lecturing. He listened and watched; he analysed the audience. He realised the extreme importance of the art: the better a scientific truth is explained and understood, the better the use that will be made of it. Faraday set out in 1813 his observations and the views he had formed in a series of long and careful letters to his friend Benjamin Abbott.

The first letter is half apologetic; here is a young bottle-washer being very critical of his distinguished superiors, but he says disarmingly, if he did not criticize, how could he learn? With that preliminary he wades straight in to his subject.

A lecturer should exert his utmost effort to gain completely the mind and attention of his audience . . . a flame should be lighted at the commencement and kept alive with unremitting splendour to the end . . . A lecturer should appear easy and collected, undaunted and unconcerned . . . and his mind clear for the contemplation and description of his subject . . . His action should not be hasty and violent, but slow, easy and natural [yet he must move about] . . . I would by no means have a lecturer glued to the table or screwed to the floor . . . The most prominent requisite to a lecturer, though perhaps really not the most important, is a good delivery: for though to all true Philosophers Science and Nature will have charms innumerable in every dress, yet I am sorry to say that the generality of mankind cannot accompany us one short hour unless the path is strewn with flowers.

However, Faraday said in later years that he could not teach and entertain at the same time.

Faraday recommends arranging thoughts on paper: 'But though I allow a Lecturer to write out his matter, I do not approve of his reading it . . . he should deliver it in a ready and free manner.' My brother W.L. Bragg, writing nearly a century and a half later, agreed about not reading a lecture.

I feel so strongly about the wrongness of reading a lecture that my language may seem immoderate. I think it is a dreadful thing to do, something quite out of keeping with all that a lecture should mean . . . The spoken word and the written word are quite different arts . . . But there are exceptions to all rules. Some very fine lecturers read their lectures, and I have tried to analyse the peculiar quality which makes their performance possible. I think they are the people who so refine and weigh every word and sentence that their beautiful prose becomes almost poetry . . . But I think one ought not to venture to read a lecture unless one has these considerable poetic gifts.

Myself I would add also the voice and manner to read it without losing contact with the audience.

To end this list of advice, here is Faraday giving a warning, picking out some examples of what he does not admire in a lecture:

A lecturer falls deeply beneath the dignity of his character when he descends so low as to angle for claps and asks for commendation. Yet I have seen a lecturer even at this point. I have heard him causelessly condemn his own powers. I have heard him dwell for a length of time on the extreme care and niceness that the experiment he will make requires. I have heard him hope for indulgence when no indulgence was wanted.

In his 'Prospectus' for setting up the RI, Rumford listed a number of subjects he thought suitable for lectures. They are distinctly domestic and well suited to the interests of the landowning Proprietors; indeed Rumford's purpose of 'teaching the application of science to the common purposes of life' does seem rather much directed to life on a great estate. These are some of the subjects:

Of the means that may be used to render Dwelling houses comfortable and salubrious.

Of the Management of Fire and the Economy of Fuel.

Of the Methods of procuring and preserving Ice in Summer, and of the best principles for constructing Ice houses.

Of the Means of cooling Liquors in hot weather, without the assistance of Ice.

Of vegetation, and the specific nature of those effects that are produced by Manure, and of the art of composing Manures adapting them to the different kinds of soil.

Of the Chemical Principles of the process of Tanning Leather.

Of the Chemical Principles of the art of making Soap, of the art of Bleaching, of the art of Dyeing [here comes the only reference to wider fields, and it is very vague] and in general of all *Mechanical Arts*, as they apply to the various branches of manufacture.

However, these kinds of subjects did not come into Garnett's programme, though some came into the list of investigations to be carried out in the laboratory, such as making bread, soup, 'research' into stoves and household furniture, into cottages and lime kilns, and 'useful machines of all descriptions'. At the same time Garnett's lectures, though they would all be scientific (whether they were on 'mechanical philosophy' or chemistry), would refer to the application of this science to the arts and manufacturers, no matter whether addressed to his fashionable, or to his more serious category of auditors. Science was tightly tied to usefulness in Rumfordian fashion, though there was less emphasis on domestic economy.

The ending of Garnett's letter to the Managers containing his proposals for lectures throws light on the behaviour of the lecture audience at the time.

With respect to a lounging room, in which they might meet before the lecture, or to which they could retire during the lecture, I assume with submission that such a place should not *on any account* be allowed. Wherever I have had accidentally such a convenient room in the vicinity of a lecture room I have been obliged to lock it up; otherwise the disturbance to the company by persons coming in or going out is intolerable.

It sounds like behaviour in the House of Commons, or how the fashionable were still behaving at the Opera in my youth.

As Garnett was giving one evening, two afternoon, and five morning lectures a week, it is not surprising that he collapsed under a load made heavier by disappointments and difficulties with the Managers.

Within the next few years it became the policy to invite outside lecturers to speak on a variety of subjects. Lectures were given in 1805–6 on music and poetry, on *belles lettres*, one on the history of Commerce, another on Zoology, on Perspective, and on Drawing in Watercolour. Mr Opie lectured on Painting and Mr Landseer (the father of Victoria's drawing master) on Engraving, only he made personal allusions and had to be asked to discontinue his course. But the preponderance of lectures were on general education in the sciences. The fashionable world flocked to the Institution. Davy's charm carried the day for chemistry, and the Revd Sydney Smith drew vast crowds to his courses on Moral Philosophy in 1804 and 1805.

A Mr Horner wrote to a Mr Murray from the Temple:

I suppose you know that Smith begins to lecture on Moral Philosophy next Saturday at the Royal Institution? You would be amused to hear the account he gives of his own qualifications for the task, and his mode of manufacturing philosophy . . . Profound metaphysics would be unsuitable for the place; he may do some good if he makes the subject amusing. He will contribute, like his other associates of the Institution, to make the real blue stockings a little more disagreeable than ever, and sensible women a little more sensible . . . When your chemists and metaphysicians in petticoats take a little general learning as an accomplishment they keep it in very tolerable order.

A very patronising view of the ladies who have always lightened the scene at the RI.

When Davy left for the Continent in 1813, Professor Brande took over the morning lectures and provided instruction in chemistry for medical students for the next forty years; Members were also allowed to attend in the latter part of the time as student numbers dropped. The lighter social side of life at the Institution was centred on Friday evenings, when Members met together in the Library for discussion and conversation: a Manager played host, and tea and coffee were served. Faraday was asked to attend and provide interesting demonstrations. In 1826 he moved the demonstrations from the Library to the Lecture Theatre and explained them: it was the start of the Friday evening Discourses. Faraday's idea was that these lectures should illustrate popular subjects and 'facilitate our object of attracting the world and making ourselves', he means the RI, 'with science attractive to it'.

1826 was a memorable year, for the Christmas Lectures 'for a Juvenile Auditory' were also started then. A few lectures for children had been tried out before, but the course of six lectures at Christmas 1826 was the first in the famous series that have gone on until the present, interrupted only during the First World War. Faraday gave

nineteen courses himself. Prince Albert brought his sons to hear
Faraday, and they wrote him thank-you letters. To attend these
lectures became a fashion for family audiences of the growing professional class.

It was the end of morning lectures and plain instruction when Brande
retired in 1852. Tyndall's advent shifted the emphasis on to research,
and the science lectures began to develop the reporting of new discoveries recently published in the Royal Society's and other scientific
journals. The Professors spoke of their own research, but Faraday only
once spoke of work as yet unpublished. That was on the famous
occasion in 1846 when Wheatstone was to lecture and, stricken with
panic at the last minute, bolted out of the building and down the street.
Faraday appeared before the waiting audience and gave as much of
Wheatstone's lecture as he could remember but, running dry before the
clock struck, began to sketch his own ideas about the research he was
then engaged on. Ever since this incident the lecturer has been watched
over by the Director, who sees him into the lecture theatre before
entering himself.

The balance between scientific and other subjects varied through the
middle of the century, as the Managers tried to provide what would be
enjoyed; the strand of 'useful science' (the arts) remained strong in the
lecture lists. Faraday lectured on an extraordinary variety of subjects in
addition to 'pure science'; on lithography and 'pure caoutchouc', on the
silvering of mirrors and dry rot, on envelope machinery and bows and
arrows. The Friday Discourses were, and have remained by tradition,
single lectures; the afternoon courses varied between two or three and
courses of ten or twelve lectures. In the 1860s geology and astronomy
were the most popular subjects; geology continued to be a great
amateur interest and there were numbers of mineral collections in
country houses (moreover the Darwin controversy in the 1860s stimulated interest in rocks). Astronomy was ever the aristocrat of the
sciences, and there were fourteen private observatories around London;
Tennyson had his own telescope at Farringford. Curiously, chemistry
and engineering were unpopular; perhaps the emerging subject of
physics had stolen some limelight from chemistry (so long so popular)
with Tyndall's dramatic lecturing. Engineering was never popular; was
engineering thought inferior to architecture, and not yet a science in its
own right? and were engineers considered socially inferior? Brunel no
doubt was a rough diamond and he never lectured at the RI; it was

Faraday who talked about Sir Marc Brunel's tunnel at Rotherhithe.

In the 1840s the lecturers had mostly been drawn from London University, from the Medical Schools in London and the Geological Survey: people for the most part living in or near London. Lecturers went the rounds and courses of lectures were almost duplicated in different places. But by the 1860s, the RI had built up a reputation for the lectures given in the best lecture theatre in London to the most distinguished audiences, and it began to be a coveted distinction to be invited to speak at the Institution. Lecturers were willing to come from a distance; the new railways brought them from Oxford and Cambridge and the north and also encouraged people to come up to London to partake of what was going on in the intellectual metropolis. There are .distinguished names in the lecture lists of the 1860s, Kelvin and Playfair, Huxley, Huggins, Crookes and Lockyer; and also some foreign names, Helmholtz and du Bois Raymond.

As the century wore on, a new need was arising; science was growing more complex, and the different scientific disciplines were drawing ever further apart, each developing its own language. There was need for some popularising in lectures to the mixed audience at the RI. Sir William Ramsay wrote to Archibald Geikie: 'The RI audience [is] the most ticklish audience in Britain to lecture before, because the most critical and the most refined, and possessing also in equal shares so much knowledge and so much ignorance.'

Times were changing rather quickly in the 1870s and 1880s. The RI had long abandoned its role of instruction and its aim of promoting 'the application of science to the arts and manufactures' had gone too (even the word 'arts' was shifting to 'fine arts' and 'technology' was taking its place). Applied science was to be learned at continuation classes in trade or technical schools of many types, joined later by polytechnics. The London Institution was losing its vocation. But the RI rode the waves and survived triumphantly by the high level of interest and 'rational entertainment' it offered and as a meeting ground for the intelligentsia of London – especially on a Friday evening. The style, the dignity, the formal procession into the theatre, the evening dress, the chatter and the array of exhibits in the impressive library – all had a part in this. But the successful club character could not have carried the RI without the reputation for research of its Professors.

The appetite that lectures satisfied was one for news; news in a variety of subjects but especially of recent scientific development and discovery. The Managers invited the men who had made the new discoveries to come and talk about it themselves. The audience saw the discoverer and heard him, feeling they were being given first hand information; felt a thrill on Friday evening when Dewar poured out his liquid air as soon as he could collect enough to pour, when Rayleigh lectured on his new discovery of argon. Members flocked to hear Preece on the new machine, the telephone, and Sir Joseph Swan on 'Electric lighting by Incandescence', or Lord Montagu of Beaulieu on 'The modern Motor-car': they crowded to hear explorers returned from their travels like Captain Speke, back in 1863 talking about his discovery of the source of the Nile. The RI was providing news and goes on providing news; I remember Leonard Woolley in the 1930s, listed to talk about his recent excavations at Ur of the Chaldees 'if he is back in time' (which he was); and in May 1981 I listened to Garry Hunt lecturing on exploration around Saturn.

How everybody packed into the lecture theatre on crowded nights is a mystery. Rumford boasted that his theatre held 900; now modern regulations on gangways only allow it to hold 452. But 1115 were squeezed in to listen to Dean Stanley (Tyndall's friend) on Westminster Abbey, and 1144 to listen to Ruskin talking about Verona. The safety of the theatre gave concern and every so often in Dewar's time a letter would appear in *The Times* pointing out its potential danger and fire risk. Nothing was done until one evening I well remember in 1928 when electric mains igniting in the street blew in the basement and blocked the only exit door from the theatre only a few hours after it had been packed with children for a Christmas lecture. A bunch of children had come up to the flat, finished our Christmas cake and stared with awe at the lecturer having tea with them. I was going out that night; I dressed early and as I stood brushing my hair on the second floor there was a terrific explosion in the street. Flames leapt past the windows and I saw something like a paving stone shoot up – it must have been the manhole cover. At the same time the lights began to flicker wildly . . . Mitcham rushed up to say we must all come down to the Theatre away from the windows: there might be more explosions. It is recorded how Mr Green, clearing up the theatre after the lecture, had smelt a sinister smell, how he and Mitcham had rushed to the basement to see black smoke issuing from under the switchroom door. Choking, they got the switches opened only just in time before there was another vast explosion in the street; part of the basement was blown in and all the ground floor windows shattered. Of course we did not know all this – we heard the glass smash while leaping flames lit the darkened flat. Everyone had to be rounded up. Fire engines clanged. Fire was raging in the manhole just outside the front door, and nobody could leave the building. We waited in the theatre thinking, 'If this had still been full of children?'

In time we were led over to Brown's Hotel where we sat in the lounge eating sandwiches, the maids, my parents and myself, still in a petticoat under a snatched-up coat. Later that night we were allowed back to a dark cold flat; and next morning I remember a workman put his pick through the water main, so there was no water either. It was a sad sight that morning: windows shattered and a black blanket of bituminous soot covering the ground floor, so that you could not tell that there were any white papers on the Newsroom tables.

It was realised immediately that major rebuilding was necessary. There was only one exit and the body of the lecture theatre was found to be separated from the gallery escape stairs only by a thin wooden partition. Plans for rebuilding were initiated at once; it was the start of a long sore job not completed until 1930.

The RI had been going through rather a doldrum period in Dewar's later years, but the lecture tradition carried on as strongly as ever. Perhaps the lectures were being given to rather more elderly audiences as lecture-going was no longer the fashionable pursuit it once had been. But formality and the stiff white shirt presented a front to the world on Friday evenings. Moreover the Christmas lectures have never failed to attract; when I was a child, the RI children's lectures, a visit to Maskelyne and Devant the conjurors, to the pantomime, or 'Gilbert and Sullivan' were parts of the entertainment of Christmas holidays in London.

The afternoon lectures which in early days had been the lively lectures for the social world were no longer well attended. Actually they had been less popular ever since the Friday Discourses became the social focus of the week. As I remember the situation in the 1920s there would only be a sprinkling of elderly ladies and fewer elderly gentlemen in the theatre to listen to some splendid afternoon lecture, and one Member often snored. My father WHB was distressed; he tried the expedient of putting on advanced scientific lectures and offering free tickets to London University students. Many remarkable scientific lectures were given in the afternoons. One venerable Member who still attends evening Discourses (and admits to an occasional drowsy moment nowadays) recalls vividly the excitement of attending in 1928 a course of lectures on wave-mechanics by Schrodinger himself, who had created the subject only about a year earlier; and how he and a colleague spent many hours after each lecture doing the 'home-work' necessary to understand this wonderful new technique which was to contribute so largely to our understanding of the structure of matter. Lectures like this helped for a time, but soon there were similar lectures being given within the University. It was the advent of war in 1939 that broke the old pattern. Then the hour of the Friday evening lectures was changed to 5 o'clock; nobody wished to be out in the black-out, but people were glad to come to listen to something that was not war news on their way home.

The afternoon courses were not revived after the war and RI afternoons were quiet until 1954 when school children began to troop in for the Schools Lectures. In an article, my brother wrote:

There is one feature about these lectures which is, in my experience, unique. The boys and girls attending each course are at the same stage in their education and so constitute an almost uniform audience. A point either goes down with all, or misses completely; an experiment excites everyone in the theatre, or falls flat so that we resolve to do it differently next day. Normally audiences include the clever and the slow, the expert and the non-expert, and one is torn between trying to suit the one or the other; this audience is 'monochromatic' and offers a most exciting challenge to the lecturer.

A technique had to be worked out for putting on lectures so lavishly illustrated by experiment; lectures repeat, and collections of apparatus assembled must be stored away from one time to the next, like the props and scenery of a repertory company. It is all very professionally done. The importance of experimental demonstration cannot be over-emphasised: W L said:

It is surprising how often people in all walks of life own that their interest in science was first aroused by attending one of these courses [here he means a Christmas lecture course] when they were young. In recalling their impressions they almost invariably say not 'we were told', but 'we were shown' this or that . . . Faraday had much to say about experiments that was very wise. The best experiments are simple and on a large scale, and their workings are obvious to the audience.

Faraday, to show magnetism, once threw a coal scuttle at his large magnet and followed it with the fire tongs. There are ways and tricks of presentation, such as to tell the audience what to look for when an experiment is to be performed so that the lecturer and audience wait, sometimes anxiously, in a togetherness, to see it come off. As WL said, 'These tricks are important because they are all part of fixing your message in the minds of the audience; they have the humble but necessary function of the hypo in fixing a photographic exposure.' And, thinking of one of those very mixed audiences often encountered at the RI or elsewhere – just the opposite of a school's lecture audience – WL observes: 'How many points can we hope to "get over" in an hour? I think the answer should be "one". If the average member of an audience can remember with interest and enthusiasm one main theme, the lecture has been a great success.' To me he put it, 'If a man can remember overnight one idea to tell his wife at breakfast . . .'

I quoted earlier in this chapter excerpts from Faraday's letters to Benjamin Abbott. Such perspicacious observations from the young man who never dreamed of being a great scientist when he was writing were gathered into a little anthology *Advice to a Lecturer* by the late Geoffrey Parr. In 1974 the anthology was republished with added 'advice' from my brother WL, drawn from his long experience (hard learned) of lecturing to children, to students, to the distinguished, the dull, the sleepy, and often at the RI to all of them together. Like Faraday, my brother studied to hold his audience, who would go home feeling they had glimpsed wonder even if they had not quite understood it all. In the new *Advice to Lecturers* the writings of the two men complement and run comfortably together.

The new outlet of television has presented new problems and opportunities. In WL's time a television lecture was a major event, especially made and recorded. He made several series for schools. The specially gathered audience was coached in behaviour beforehand, the lecturer was made up, and the operators rushed about making last arrangements to coils of wire while cameras were manoeuvred and adjusted in position, the lecture assistant Bill Coates watching his apparatus anxiously. And then it was GO. WL with winning enthusiasm started – but, 'Just a minute, Sir Lawrence', and he was stopped while a camera or something was moved a fraction: then a new start. 'It was so hard', WL used to say, 'to go on making "fresh" starts when it might be the fourth or fifth, or to have to repeat "sudden" ideas or impromptu remarks.' Sometimes half a lecture had to be re-recorded. Once he was asked to do the repeat weeks later, and of course, to wear

Sir William H. Bragg

Sir Henry Dale

Sir Eric Rideal

E. N. da C. Andrade

W. L. Bragg giving Schools Lecture, 1963

the same clothes for it; but in the meantime his wife had sent his suit to a village jumble sale. The buyer was tracked, but she had only bought the jacket, the trousers had vanished. The re-take was done with WL standing close to the lecture table so that it was not obvious that the trousers only nearly matched the jacket.

Sir George Porter has developed widely the new possibilities offered by television, and the professional broadcasters have refined their techniques (as will be recorded at greater length in Chapter 9). Now the Christmas lectures can be given and televised live without special arrangements or hitch, and are watched by hundreds of thousands of 'Juveniles' who could never have got up to London to hear them. Such arts have been practised in the lecture theatre as part of the RI's special aim to try and keep the different subjects, different cultures in touch, and above all to try to explain science to the non-scientist, for, as WL put it:

I believe it is our duty . . . to render an account of our stewardship which is readily understood by our fellow men who are intelligent and shrewd, although they may not be familiar with all our technical terms. Further, the conveying of scientific ideas to people who are not specialists is a fascinating art which deserves all respect. It is only to be learnt by bitter experience of making many mistakes, and by intensive study. The wide diffusion of knowledge about science is so very important that the art of doing so is well worth learning.

Certainly, it has been well studied at the Royal Institution.

EIGHT

The Royal Institution
and Education

DIFFUSION of knowledge has been the aim of the RI from its very beginning; so many of Rumford's hopes and plans for the Institution were transformed, but this one never. It has only changed character from time to time. This spreading of knowledge has always been by lecture, and the art of lecturing, as described in the last chapter, was studied and practised and refined till it has become at the RI an exquisite means of education. It has varied of course, depending on whether the lecturing has been to artisans, to 'fashion', for serious students, for those who came for some interest and more entertainment, for the expert, or for children. Sometimes the Institution's ideas have been too modern for their day, and at other times it has not done much at all; sometimes the contribution has been a prophet's call from a professor; always there has been education offered in the widest sense of opening minds, of keeping touch and of rousing wonder.

> Knowledge can only wonder breed
> And not to know is wonder's seed

Wonder is a quality of the good life. 'The training that is got here, the learning to sit and try and understand, is something which is of great value in life', was the way old Sir James Dewar put it.

While the RI has to this day provided a mixed fare for general interest, more direct or formal instruction has always been in the sciences. The Christmas Juvenile lectures have always been scientific, for science is the RI's real business.

One can recognise three strands in the Institution's educational purpose:

1 Education in the widest sense of rousing interest, spreading knowledge and keeping touch between disciplines

2 Direct science instruction

3 The efforts by RI professors to promote education and especially science education in the country at large

These strands are woven together through the Institution's history.

In the early years, the first strand of wide culture was catered for in the afternoon lectures for the gentlemen and their ladies, those people to whom, as Garnett said, 'I hope we shall be able to communicate considerable knowledge without any trouble to themselves'. There is the slight contempt of the specialist for the amateur in his remark and one must admit they were amateurs, but the best of them were fine ones. They were the top people, educated in the plan of the 'comprehensive education' of an 18th-century gentleman; much of it may have been O level or A level knowledge, but of a wide span. Educated probably at home by a tutor, they learned science as well as classics and mathematics. The tutor possibly accompanied them to Oxford or Cambridge, and then on the Grand Tour where they discovered art, learned languages and acquired polish. Perhaps it was the best balanced education that has been attempted for the few. The total sum of knowledge made such a comprehensive ideal conceivable then. In Chapter 2 I noted Thomas Young's marvellous accomplishments and the long list of subjects Davy set himself to master. In the late 1790s Coleridge devised an unrealistic scheme for an 'ideal school' in which he planned to teach 'complete knowledge' of subjects which included the sciences as well as most other known fields of study. We can see that it was an impossible goal; but the ideal of the gentleman with all-round knowledge remains a very civilised conception. The scientific explosion in the late 17th century and the founding of the Royal Society had given impetus to a gentlemanly interest in science. In the relatively stable 18th century such appetites for knowledge led to the growth of the first Literary and Philosophical Societies in provincial cities. It was this wide interest in just about everything, and especially in science, that the RI was intended to cater for, with the concern for philanthropy and reform (coupled with agricultural self-interest) tipping the balance in favour of the new excitement of applied science.

In the 19th century specialised societies began to absorb the function of many of the old Literary and Philosophical Societies; but at the RI the scientific research which became so important by mid century has been the lifeblood which has kept alive and strong the old tradition of wide culture. May it always do so; it is so necessary. The scientist must listen to the Arts (using the word in its present sense, not as Rumford and his early successors used it, meaning what we call crafts). My brother W.L. Bragg when he was Cavendish Professor at Cambridge organised a weekly Arts Lecture for his Honours students; it was voluntary, but they flocked to it. He was deeply hurt that the Arts Faculties wanted no Science lectures for their people. Everyone should ask 'why' about the world they live in, and be ready to listen to some answers from Science – even Arts people. Perhaps they are more ready now, but science is so difficult and scientists are not always good at explaining. Hence the value of the good 'popular' book: my father, WHB, was always ready to put infinite trouble into his 'popular' lectures or books, for it was his creed that science was not just for the specialist, but that some understanding of what science has to tell should be a basic equipment for life. A most important opportunity was lost at Oxford in mid-19th century when there was some pressure from outside that more science should be introduced into the University. A proposal by Henry Acland (Reader in Anatomy) that some science should be part of every student's study was thrown out. It would be a waste of time, some said. This was one of the beginnings of the great rift between the cultures. It is a fascinating thought that Oxford might have instituted a basic general knowledge of science for its undergraduates; what might this have meant for the country? Meantime the old RI has gone on doing its best to keep a link, and this constitutes what I have called the first strand of RI education, spreading knowledge in the widest sense.

The second category, second strand, has been instruction for those whom Garnett described as 'attached to scientific pursuits'. He proposed a full course of experimental philosophy for them, five mornings a week. Out of this has grown, been checked and has redeveloped the RI contribution to systematic education of the more formal kind: but before trying to assess what has been achieved at the RI it is well to look at the educational position outside.

Reviewing the country as a whole and passing beyond the élite who relied on tutors for their education (or occasionally on exceptional parents), we can say that middle class boys went either to one of the few old schools such as Eton, Winchester, Harrow or St Pauls (very unruly before the 1830s) or to run-down grammar schools where they got classics and maths, but no science unless they were dissenters. The dissenters fared better, for their schools and academies were more vigorous and modern in outlook, providing some science. Many boys went to them who were not dissenters, but after Arnold's leadership had spread through public schools (which were nearly all Anglican) the proportionate influence of the dissenting schools declined. Few in the working class got any formal education beyond the three Rs at a charity or Sunday school. Meanwhile the Industrial Revolution was breeding a new type of artisan, the technicians who must mind and service the new machinery of Industry. These were forced to try and absorb technical science either from itinerant lecturers or from the Mechanics Institutes which were springing up by the second quarter of the 19th century. It was this gap between primary and technical education which worried Tyndall so much, and led to outspoken comments by Prince Albert who contrasted conditions here with the organised system of education which was being built up in the German states and led from Primary School right up to State University. Dewar was still harping on the same theme in his presidential address to the British Association in 1902:

To my mind the appalling thing is not that the Germans have seized this or the other industry . . . it is that the German population has reached a point of general training . . . which it will take us two generations of hard and intelligently directed educational work to attain. It is that Germany possesses a natural weapon of precision which must give her an enormous initial advantage in any contest depending upon disciplined and methodical intellect.

Inter-state rivalry had boosted the German system: many German states supported well equipped laboratories such as the famous Liebig laboratory, privately started but carried forward by the State. British chemists all through the century went to study in Germany, and we in turn imported German chemists to teach in our universities and fill posts in British industry. By contrast, in England all through the 19th century many workmen joined the technical trades without any train- ing at all. Most organised training was through apprenticeship, by learning on the job from one who knew the traditional method but was usually ignorant of the scientific reasons behind it. Although he is unwise who despises handed-down knowledge because of an unscientific explanation, this system does not easily accept scientific research and development.

'Self-help' became a by-word and almost a craze in 19th century Britain, and did something to make up for the gaps in education. *Self-Help with Illustrations of Conduct and Performance* by Samuel Smiles was published in 1859. About the same time Lord Brougham's 'Society for the Diffusion of Useful Knowledge' was beginning to turn out cheap books on science and technology by tens of thousands. Self-help-with-God-helping-those-who-help-themselves and an emphasis on Christian character helped Britain to muddle through. But there is no real virtue in 'muddling through', though the British are inclined to condone and be slightly amused at it; it is leaving rather too much to God.

Here the State did little to organise British education through most of the 19th century, apart from giving a little money for buildings. 'Laissez faire' policy prevailed, understandably while the Government did not dare to fund Church or Dissenting schools for fear of offending the one or the other. State-supported primary schools were established in 1870 and secondary education only followed in 1902. Meanwhile mechanics institutes, trade schools, technical schools and polytechnics (initially of several types) were springing up seemingly at random; but (as my father WHB said in a report he made on English education in 1897) for lack of proper grounding the money spent on technical education was largely thrown away. Prince Albert's warning had not been heeded.

This is the background against which the teaching provided by the RI during the 19th century must be viewed; the more formal teaching that I have called the second strand in the RI's educational effort.

As well as the morning lectures for those 'seriously interested in scientific pursuits' there was in the beginning Webster's short lived School for Mechanics. I have described its fortunes in Chapter 1. Here I want to stress how forward looking, how modern was his scheme. Webster wrote to Rumford with his proposal for the school in September 1799, pointing out that lack of scientific knowledge among mechanics hindered the development of mechanical inventions. He then described what he planned to teach them: first, plane geometry and some architectural drawing (Webster was having great trouble at the time with workmen engaged on the RI alterations who could not understand his plans). Students were then to proceed to the principles of mechanics and hydrostatics. After that they were to specialize: the builders to study architecture, those who would mind machinery to study higher mathematics, natural philosophy and chemistry. Note that he was running into the problem of the later mechanics institutes, still later polytechnics: how to teach higher mathematics to a man only equipped with the three Rs? But Webster inspired by experience at Anderson's in Glasgow, had put his finger on a need; his abortive school was a forerunner in the south of Britain, and incidentally foreshadowed a 20th century development. His students were to be workmen released from their jobs to follow a course, thus anticipating the block-release courses of today. One must salute Webster; whether his school might have been successful if it had managed to circumvent the anti-Jacobin suspicion of educating the working class, it is impossible to guess. Writing an account of his scheme many years later in 1837, Webster claimed that his attempt anticipated the work of Dr Birkbeck in founding the London Mechanics Institution in 1823. Webster's idea was like a plant put out too early in spring that got nipped by the frost.

Another suggestion for a training school came from the East India Company in 1802; some knowledge of science would help in the development of their trade. Could the RI run a training school for some of their employees? Although to teach the sons of nabobs was not dangerous like teaching artisans, the Managers turned down the idea. However, Davy and later Faraday were both given permission to take private pupils in the laboratory. Once a lady wrote to Faraday asking if she might come to study and offering to go through all his experiments with him; he wrote her a long and charming letter in reply, gently refusing.

Davy's lecturing had provided much sound instruction laced with charm; with Brande installed in Davy's place in 1813 the teaching became more formal and systematic. Davy could never be systematic, but Brande had students to equip for a medical career, and for several decades the RI did play an integral part in medical training in London. There was no special syllabus, medical students at that time were merely required to show attendance at a sufficiently large number of chemistry lectures. Brande was conscientious, practical if a little dull, and aimed at training the 'compleat' practical chemist. Bence Jones went to his lectures, as did Sir Frederick Pollock the eminent lawyer who became such a figure at the RI and whose memoirs I have quoted.

After 1848 Members were admitted to these lectures, since student numbers were dropping as hospitals began to provide chemistry teaching in their own medical schools. When Brande retired in 1853 the morning laboratory lectures came to an end; there was no longer the same need for them. In the early years of the century the RI had been the best place to learn experimental science, but University College London had been offering science courses since the late 1820s; and in 1845 the Royal College of Chemistry came into being.

The College of Chemistry grew out of an idea for yet another training school at the RI, put forward in 1843. There was great interest in chemistry at the time, and great hopes for its practical application in two special directions. One was a revival of chemistry to help agriculture; the interest in Davy's agricultural chemistry had rather died down in the days of comparative prosperity for farming under the protective Corn Laws, and the old Board of Agriculture was no more. But in the early forties agitation for repeal of the Corn Laws was rising and farmers were getting anxious; every opportunity for improvement that agricultural chemistry offered should be explored, and the writings of Liebig (the German organic chemist) recently translated into English showed English agriculturalists how Germany as usual was forging ahead.

But it was in the realm of medicine that chemistry might play an even greater part, so it was thought. Scientific medicine was the thing of the moment, for problems of public health multiplied with the crowding urban populations – problems of water supply and sewage disposal, bad housing and disease. So many children died in the slums; Victorian poems and stories are full of death. Dickens wrote his novels to open people's eyes to the evils of the time as he daily battled in person against them. George Eliot in *Middlemarch* describes the young doctor, Mr Lydgate, ardent to reform medical practice with the new ideas of 'scientific medicine'.

The proposal for the School of Practical Chemistry at the RI was put forward by the Society of Apothecaries. Apothecaries were trying to raise themselves from the lowest medical grade to a profession, and to go through a course at the RI would both teach expertise and raise status. Brande welcomed the idea of a school, and Faraday was agreeable if it could be done well; but after closer examination both advised that space within the Institution was already so filled by the growing stock of apparatus, minerals and books that it appeared impracticable to introduce the proposed school in addition, and the Managers rejected the request with regret. Instead, and largely by effort of the apothecaries, the College of Chemistry was founded. It became the Royal College in 1853 and later on was affiliated to the Royal School of Mines which in turn became part of Imperial College.

When Brande retired, his assistant, Professor Brodie, wished to carry on, but he wanted to give more advanced lectures; the Managers demurred and Brodie, disappointed, retired also. However, Tyndall carried on a link with medicine by his afternoon lectures. They were not courses designed for students, but his lectures were popular with the doctors, who bought tickets for single courses; young officers came too, from Woolwich and Chatham, where Faraday had lectured and Tyndall was examining candidates for commissions. But such lectures faded out when Dewar came; and nearly fifty years later my father W.H. Bragg's attempt to attract Honours students from London University to the RI by offering advanced science lectures soon withered when such lectures became available within the University. It was the old pattern repeating, of the RI filling a need until it was fulfilled elsewhere.

In the Second World War, plainly instructional courses were organised which were perhaps serving a war need rather than being a function of the RI. WHB taught electricity to Air Cadets, young boys training to fill the wasting numbers of the Royal Air Force.

In sorting out the two strands in the Institution's educational purposes, I have not included the Juvenile Christmas lectures in either; they really belong to both, for they have brought delight and interest to the young of all ages, and taught science visually through superb experimental demonstration. It was in 1826 that Faraday started the series, but lectures for children had been tried out before; there was a notice in *The Times* of 17 December 1825:

Royal Institution of Great Britain, Albemarle St, Dec 5th 1825. A wish having been expressed by several of the Members that a Course of lectures be delivered at the Royal Institution in the Christmas and other vacations on some of the leading branches of Natural Philosophy adapted to the comprehension of a Juvenile Auditory the Managers announce ... that John Millington Esq, FRS, Secretary Astronomical Society, Professor of Mechanics to the Royal Institution, will *deliver a course of twenty-two lectures* on the various branches of Experimental Philosophy ...

The course was to be spread over the Christmas and Whitsuntide vacations. But the Managers must have decided that so long a course filling so much holiday time was too much for the young; six lectures at Christmas are the right ration. Faraday gave nineteen courses in all, and his lectures are a superb example of what science should be taught and how it should be presented to the young, leading them from contemplation of familiar objects to the powers of the Universe.

The Schools Lectures, that have now been going for nearly thirty years, follow in this tradition, but they are designed to fit in with school science. Lectures are given for 6th-form and 4th-form pupils, also some for preparatory school children. Representatives of the Headmasters and Headmistresses Association advise on lecture programmes and schools mainly apply for tickets through the education authorities. Each talk, four times repeated, is thus heard by about 2000 children who are brought by their teachers from schools in London and the Home Counties, and from even further afield. The great idea is to show in these lectures experiments that could never be mounted at school; and the children often have a chance to inspect and sometimes even handle equipment as well. It is a great way of teaching and learning; as my brother W.L. Bragg said, such lectures encourage the practical bent which, by employing all the faculties, enables a British student to compete successfully with Continental students who have more text book learning. WL also catered for the interests and needs of the teachers by inviting them to the Institution for research days to hear a talk by the head of some research school, meet with members of his team and discuss with them work which otherwise they would only read about – when teachers have time to read.

The third strand in the RI's contribution to education I tried to define at the start of this chapter as the efforts of its Professors to promote the cause of education and especially science education in the country at large. With Tyndall established as Professor of Natural Philosophy in 1853, research became the main objective at the Institution, coupled with exposition; but if the RI no longer provided systematic teaching in the 1850s and 1860s, it was giving a great boost to the drive for science education. This was a topical subject among the intelligentsia. There was still a dearth of science in grammar and public schools, and much discussion as to how to introduce it into the curriculum. Faraday and

Tyndall were both ardent educationalists. With Tyndall, furthering science in schools was part of his campaign to promote science as a profession and gain Government support for it.

In 1854, the RI Managers discovered that the Royal Society of Arts was putting on a course of lectures on educational subjects. The Institution could not be outdone; Bence Jones hurriedly organized seven lectures on Science and Education. The lectures were given by 'seven great guns' as Tyndall described them. He was one of them himself, and others included Whewell, Master of Trinity College Cambridge, Professor Daubeny from Oxford, and Faraday. Bence Jones considered the series so important that he had them published in book form and distributed to all the Institution's Members.

Whewell's theme was the influence of science on education; he set out examples to show that every great advance in intellectual education has been the effect of scientific discovery in the previous period. Daubeny, 'On the Importance of Chemistry', argued how chemistry developed (and how desirable it was so to develop in the young) the faculty of minutely observing, of clearly apprehending, and of correctly classifying the objects that present themselves. This was the aspect for which John Ruskin respected science. Faraday's title was 'Observations on Mental Education', and is the most interesting and important of the set, for it tells so much about himself. As a young man he had had to find his own path through the forests of knowledge towards scientific discovery; his own education was a supreme example of 'Self-Help' long before the time of Samuel Smiles. Isaac Watts in his *Improvement of the Mind* had given Faraday a clue, and Faraday stuck for life to the way that he had mapped out in his early days. In his lecture in 1854 he spoke of the scientific quest; of the Hypothesis, suggested by the Imagination, which must be tested by Experiment; and of the experimental evidence which must be checked by Judgement. Faraday was ever urging the necessity of judgement to a society whose gullibility over Spiritualism infuriated him. To cultivate the judgement should be a prime object of education. Faraday was not only thinking of the path of the scientific researcher; this is a way of dealing with life applicable to Everyman, the explorer's way of advancing into unknown country, into tomorrow.

Faraday believed with his whole heart that science should share place with the wisdom of the ancients and the logic of mathematics in the training of young minds. For decades the controversy over science teaching dragged on and in 1862 Faraday spoke out almost impatiently to the Public School Commissioners, saying:

That the natural knowledge which has been given to the world in such abundance during the last fifty years should remain untouched, and that no sufficient attempt should be made to convey it to the young mind growing up and obtaining its first view of these things is to me a matter so strange that I find it difficult to understand. Though I think I see the opposition breaking away, it is yet a hard one to overcome. That it ought to be overcome I have not the least doubt in the world.

But how was the teaching to be done, even if agreed to? There were not the teachers. 'If there be one profession in England of paramount importance, I believe it to be the teacher', Tyndall declared in his one of the seven lectures which he called 'On the Importance of the Study of Physics as a branch of Education for all Classes'. He was the only one of the seven who had taught in school and knew how little experience there was on how to present science in class. There was also the jealousy of the entrenched classics masters to cope with.

In 1861 Bence Jones wrote to the headmasters of half-a-dozen public schools to find out how much science was actually being offered at each of them. Montagu Butler replied that, 'The study of Natural Philosophy does not form part of the ordinary work of boys at Harrow. It is compulsory on no one.' However, a prize book might be won by taking an exam. From Winchester Dr Moberly reported that ten or twelve science lectures were given each year at which everyone attended, but there was no exam. This was explained in a polite reply to Bence Jones; but on another occasion Moberly expressed the view, 'that for a school like Winchester, science is useless'. From Eton Dr Goodford wrote to say that there was one course of lectures offered in the Michaelmas term; attendance was voluntary, averaging one hundred boys. There was no mention in any letter of a laboratory or experimental work. One does not feel that science had more than a toe in the door of these great schools.

If intellectual society was losing interest in science as the century advanced it was only partly because science had grown harder to understand; it was also because men who had been to public schools were not so well equipped to understand it as their tutor-educated grandfathers. I believe that the Victorian headmasters are responsible for a lot. The sons of the landed gentry, of professional men, of industrialists passed through their hands with the result that generations grew up, most of them lacking any knowledge of what science was about and, what is worse, rather despising it, although they would be admirably equipped to run an Empire or man a Civil Service.

By the first quarter of the 20th century there had occurred a certain down-grading of science and scientists; it became socially acceptable for persons to proclaim an ignorance of science who would not have dared to say they knew nothing of music or literature or art. And this down-grading tendency was aggravated by a question of class, for rather a high proportion of scientists at that period were not 'Public School' themselves and had not been to Oxford or Cambridge, but to London or one of the provincial universities or a polytechnic. It is also true that bright boys whose background did not favour their development in one of the older disciplines were attracted to science, for there they might succeed; and, in their turn, they often lacked respect for the humanities.

So it came about that science was not quite 'U' in the Mitford sense for some while, until the public schools began to give grudging welcome to science, and science gradually became worthy of a serious place in the gentleman's education once again. By now science is everywhere essential, whether liked or not; I think it is the conception of 'the gentleman' that is less sure.

Probably the great block to science teaching at public schools in the last century was that Oxford and Cambridge offered no degrees in Natural Science for so long. However Whewell, Master of Trinity, got Prince Albert elected as Chancellor of the University and, with Albert's influence, managed to get the Science Tripos established at Cambridge in 1858. The scientists may have dubbed Albert 'the Royal Gull', but there is no doubt that he was very useful to them and the cause of science. The Cavendish Laboratory was founded in 1872, with Clerk-Maxwell and Lord Rayleigh as its first Professors. All the same, the Mathematics Tripos remained pre-eminent, and until around the end of the century Cambridge men approached science via mathematics; it is a good international language.

It was not only the hold of classics that retarded the introduction of science and history at the old universities; the Anglican church had strong influence through the denominational bar to students, which was not lifted till 1871. Fellows mostly took Orders (at some colleges they had to); science especially was in disgrace with the Church after the Darwin scandal. The effect was passed on to the public schools where headmasters were often College Fellows and clergymen as well.

Faraday had urged science teaching; Tyndall fought for it and for the position of science in the country; Thomas Huxley was a third RI Professor engaged in the campaign. He battled for science in school and for education generally with such unremitting energy that his early scientific promise hardly had time to fulfil itself. Darwin's protagonist, Huxley fought for scientific truth with a Victorian confidence that he knew just what it was. He blasted religious obscurantism and coined the word 'agnostic'; especially he threw himself into the cause of adult education for the working man. Both he and Tyndall lectured to artisans at the Royal School of Mines in Jermyn Street. Huxley lectured also at the Working Men's College founded by F.D. Maurice, where Ruskin and Kingsley also taught. Huxley became Principal of the South London Working Men's College and one of the first Governors of the London School Board after 1870.

When Dewar took over the RI effort in the cause of education died down. He complained about English education in his 1902 British Association address, but did little to further it. There was a hiatus for nearly fifty years until my father W.H. Bragg picked up the trumpet from the dust. When WHB came to the RI in 1923 he had already been campaigning for education for half a lifetime, in fact since he arrived in Australia in 1886 and found his students at Adelaide University so poorly grounded. In 1888 the shy young Professor, aged 26, gave the University Commemoration Address on Education, speaking out bluntly and pleading, 'for good general education with experimental science' in the curriculum. Ten years later he returned 'home' (to England) on a year's sabbatical leave with a commission from the South Australian Government to study education in England and on the Continent; as a result of his report it was laid down that all prospective elementary school teachers in S. Australia had to follow a year's (free) course at the University before they could qualify. Back in England, at Leeds, WHB lectured to the Workers Educational Association; later, in London, he was President of the Science Masters Association. Schools were offering science more and more seriously. One can see the progression at Winchester: in 1854 Moberly had scorned science; in 1872 another headmaster, Dr Ridding, sent for his maths master Mr Croft, said 'I think we might teach the boys a little science', and sent Mr Croft back to Oxford to read physics. In 1904 the science block was built. By the 1930s the science masters no longer occupied the lowest place in common rooms. WHB opened new laboratories at schools, spreading his creed of 'help your neighbour' with science as a tool for the job. Old Thomas Bernard would have approved.

In the first quarter of this century it had always been a battle to get more science into schools, but towards the thirties there appeared a new twist. The quantity of young scientists produced had greatly increased, but in the rush, especially at the new universities and polytechnics, they were being reared on too much science at the cost of the humanities. These young men could be a little brash, somewhat contemptuous of all but science, and ill equipped to explain themselves and their findings to the world. WHB claimed that, 'the humanities and science were not rivals but companions, and neither could grow without the other', and he campaigned to redress a balance. To the English Association he stressed how vital it was to teach a fine use of words, so that the laboratory worker might be able to explain himself to his boss, and so that the research worker could write a precise description. It is said of Einstein that it was his fine use of words in descriptions that helped his revolutionary ideas to gain acceptance in the first instance, and that he had learned such exact use of words as a young man when he was employed to write descriptive reports on applications for patents of technical inventions. WHB went further, saying that the better a new idea was described, the better was the chance of it being well used.

After WHB's time, the RI again housed no active educationalist until my brother W.L. Bragg went there: Sir Henry Dale was war-time caretaker, Sir Eric Rideal too busy trying to re-organize after the war, Professor Andrade much too busy trying to reform the Institution. But the Schools lectures that my brother had the imagination to start revived the whole teaching aim of the RI in full force.

It had been the constant aim of my father that all children should grow up equipped with a basic general knowledge of science; how this was still not happening is illustrated by a quaint development in my brother's time at the RI. In the late 1950s the heads of the Civil Service were getting worried that, in an age depending on science, their administrators knew little of what science was about. The RI offered its help, and in May 1964 the Chief Secretary to the Treasury announced to the House of Commons that, 'a course of lectures and seminars in science subjects for members of the Administrative class [of the Civil Service] is being arranged at the Royal Institution of Great Britain. The aim of these lectures is to give administrators an introduction to the fundamental laws of science and some ideas of scientific methodology.' It was not an easy job to organize elementary lectures that would be tactful to the dignity of mature Civil Servants. The first course which started in October 1964 was exploratory, and revealing. By the next year a pattern had been worked out and it was made part of these administrators' working week to attend a course of 18 lectures on 9 successive Thursday mornings. Results were fairly successful, but as WLB said, 'the main trouble is that of trying to concentrate the whole of science into 9 mornings with a class that on the whole has no scientific background' – a technique very different from that of the Schools Lectures. Probably any teenager of the time who enjoyed space fiction and fiddling with radios would have known more than these gentlemen did. Certainly in the 1980s, television-reared children who will learn to use computers may laugh at the amusing ignorance of the old generation; but I hope these children will also learn to explain our difficulties to us in exact, fine, lucid English.

Sir W. Lawrence Bragg

Delivery of diamond synthesiser
before Discourse on 2 May, 1974

Sir George Porter

H.M. The Queen opening the Faraday
Museum and laboratory in 1973
(see p. 156)

NINE

The Royal Institution Today

GEORGE PORTER

by Alban Caroe

I HAVE NOW to take up the narrative which Gwendy Caroe dropped at the end of Chapter 6. When W.L. Bragg retired from being Director in 1966 the Royal Institution may still have seemed very like what it had been thirty years earlier, when his father was there with the prestige of being President of the Royal Society, and before the Second War had broken the continuity of life in London. The building was almost unaltered (except in the Director's flat); young scientists in the Davy–Faraday closely resembled their predecessors in their pride and delight in the search for new knowledge in closely related subjects; and full evening dress was still worn at Discourses. But the RI under WLB's leadership had done more than just emerge successfully from a storm; great and important new developments had been achieved during the second half of those thirty years. New links had been forged between Science and Industry by the creation of the category of Corporate Subscribers whose attendance revitalised mutual interests as well as providing much-needed financial support for the Institution; a significant contribution had been made towards raising the standard of scientific education for the young, as children in their hundreds flocked into the building for the afternoon Schools Lectures; and the fascination of good scientific demonstration was being spread widely through the nation by films and by televising RI lectures reproduced with increasing dexterity. After Professor George Porter came into residence as Director in 1966 (Sir George in 1972) all these developments were speeded up, and many others were added to them.

Following precedents set earlier in this book, something must be written about Sir George's previous experience. After passing as a scholar through Leeds University studying physical chemistry and chemical kinetics, he joined the RNVR to work on Radar. The training in electronics and pulse techniques gained in the Navy proved useful later in suggesting new approaches to chemical problems. From 1945 to

1949 he worked under Professor Norrish in the Physical Chemistry Department at Cambridge University, studying free radicals produced in gaseous photochemical reactions. Becoming first a Demonstrator and then Assistant Director of Research in Physical Chemistry, also Fellow of Emmanuel College, he turned his attention to wider applications of flash photolysis methods, to diverse problems of physics, chemistry and biology. In 1955 Porter moved to Sheffield, starting as Professor of Physical Chemistry and subsequently becoming Head of the Department of Chemistry. He was elected Fellow of the Royal Society in 1960. His work on the study of extremely fast chemical reactions effected by disturbing the equilibrium by means of very short pulses of energy' gained him a Nobel Prize. This was in 1967, shortly after he arrived at the RI, and was awarded jointly to him and to two others, one of whom was the Professor Norrish already mentioned. Porter had earlier been elected to the (visiting) professorship of Chemistry at the RI in 1963, having lectured there regularly since 1960.

The developments which have been taking place with increasing tempo since 1966 have been spread over all aspects of the RI's activities. This book has been devoted to tracing the slow unfolding of those activities, but Sir George Porter has redefined their aims with such greater precision that it is worth following his lead and restating them here. The present aims of the Royal Institution are to advance:

1 Scientific research
2 Education – both by direct instruction especially of the young, and also by inspiring all listeners and thereby spreading knowledge
3 The Social or Club aspect of a society of Members who have 'a knowledge or a love of Science'. Many of them are not professional scientists. Their interests spread potentially into all branches of learning, and one of their important responsibilities is the maintenance of a building which has the longest history of scientific achievement of any in Britain.

All these are interlocked; but it is worth examining each of them separately, and this division will be followed through the rest of this chapter.

Though crystallographic research work continued in the Davy–Faraday Laboratory after the 1966 change in Directors, arrangements had been made for most X-ray crystallographers to move elsewhere, as already reported in Chapter 6. Professor Porter's team was therefore able to move in without delay and to continue in Albemarle Street their researches into the interaction of light with molecules and into the consequent fast reactions and transient intermediate states. Much of their work has been on various aspects of flash photolysis, which the non-scientist can think of as meaning the excitation or decomposition of molecules by flashes of incredibly short duration, sometimes repeated at very short intervals; those durations having been progressively shortened through the years from microseconds (millionths of a second) to picoseconds (millionths of a millionth of a second), first using ordinary light, then lasers, and then 'mode-locked pulse trains'. Another research still being pursued has been the so-far-incomplete attempt to emulate and perhaps improve upon the ability of plants to use chlorophyll to photosynthesise carbohydrates or other fuels from water and carbon dioxide in the atmosphere, and thus provide the energy needed to sustain life. If that research succeeds, the economic manufacture and storage of stable chemical fuels may become possible, enabling the world to compensate for shortages of gas, oil and coal, and reduce dependence on nuclear fuels with their attendant dangers. Further lines of research have been developed since 1980 when David Phillips joined the Davy–Faraday in the newly established Wolfson Professorship of Natural Philosophy. He heads a second photochemistry research group which also uses short pulses of laser light to study rapid changes in large molecules, including polymers and substances of biological importance as well as gaseous molecules at temperatures within one degree of the absolute zero.

But the DF laboratories have not been given over solely to pure research; they have also seen the start of an interesting new venture in scientific development. A private company, wholly owned at first by the RI and called Applied Photophysics Limited, was started there in 1971 to develop and manufacture scientific instruments needed in the first place for work in the Davy–Faraday, such as flash photolysis equipment. It proved so successful that it has not only been able to make welcome contributions to the RI finances but has also increased sufficiently in size to make it necessary to move the APL workshops away from Albemarle Street, though its contract research subsidiary (Photophysics Research Ltd) remains in No. 20. Interestingly patents arising have not generated any litigation of the kind in which Dewar was so frequently involved.

*   *   *

We turn now to the second aspect of the Institution's activities – Education – where we are in effect writing a postscript to Chapter 8, and concentrating initially on direct instruction to the young. That is where the most heart-warming effects of formal education can often be found. Great flexibility has been shown in selecting the methods of education best suited to the RI's capabilities: new subjects have been introduced; greater involvement by pupils has been sought; and efforts have been made in several ways to extend the guidance offered beyond the limits of one building or one area. Consequently this section includes a number of diverse activities.

Children of three age groups continue to flood into the RI for the afternoon Schools Lectures started by W.L. Bragg, and his methods of teaching by demonstration have been more widely appreciated since a series of sixteen of his lectures was filmed in colour and published with accompanying teaching notes. The popularity of these Schools Lectures is now very firmly established. Moreover means have been found to spread the influence of the RI's efforts to improve the standards of teaching science to children beyond the limitations of what is possible within a single building. Three-day Science Seminars have been held in various parts of the country aimed at attracting children who have not yet taken their O-levels. The first day is spent at the RI touring historical rooms, inspecting modern research laboratories, and being entertained by two demonstration lectures. The children then spend two subsequent days in laboratories in their own area, carrying out experiments at their own pace. Such Seminars have been held in various places in the Home Counties and as far afield as Cardiff; all have been repeated by the schools themselves, and the local authorities in other districts are now following.

A new development was inaugurated when a pilot series of ten Mathematics Master Classes for Young People was held in the RI on consecutive Saturday mornings early in 1981, attended by sixty 12–13-year-olds drawn from Inner London, Hertfordshire and the National Association for Gifted Children. Enthusiasm was intense and showed in the constant high level of attendances. In consequence these have become a biennial activity at the RI and a number of similar Master Classes have been organised in other parts of the country, including Cambridge, Warwickshire, Birmingham, Suffolk, Sussex and Edinburgh. Most are to be repeated and further centres are planned elsewhere. The necessary financial support has been obtained from various sources often extending over a 3-year period. In 1984 the first set of Physics Master Classes was held at the University of Sussex, planned on similar lines in co-operation with the RI, the final item in the programme being a demonstration lecture in the Institution itself followed by visits to the Faraday Museum and laser laboratories.

In 1967 the Royal Institution, at the invitation of the Science Foundation for Physics within the University of Sydney, took a hand in linking Britain to international efforts to widen the outlook of promising scientific scholars by sending five British sixth-formers to spend two weeks at the International Science School in Sydney, and this has continued regularly since. The British contingents are known as the 'Royal Institution Science Scholars'; they are accompanied by an escort; while in Sydney they join with scholars from other countries (mainly from the United States, Australia, New Zealand and Japan); they visit interesting places on their journeys out and back, and are invited to a Garden Party at Buckingham Palace before leaving. The Association for Science Education has taken a prominent share with the RI in organising this venture from Britain and in the very careful procedures adopted for selecting suitable scholars, chosen not only for their academic performances but also for width of interests, personality and likelihood of being 'good ambassadors'. Escorts report that the scholars take the lectures they attend most seriously, and join actively in the scientific meetings and discussions which are interspersed. Lodged as they are with Australian families, most scholars also become immersed in a whirl of social gaiety, making friendly contacts with many circles in many countries. On the social side some of the more staid escorts have been surprised how small an impression the beauties and special interests of the places they visit seem to make upon the young people; there seems to be a tendency to meet every new experience in (say) Washington, Sydney or Bangkok with 'almost the same excited enthusiasm as might be evoked by a successful fairground in England'. The Australians are reported to value highly the contacts which these academic visits make possible. These scholarships continue to be granted in alternate years, but the RI has been forced to reduce its efforts to raise financial support.

The Institution has also tried to raise the level of science teaching for the young by offering specialist help for science teachers. Two efforts in this direction provide interesting lessons, for both withered away after promising beginnings. Both were started by W.L. Bragg, much helped by Professor Ronald King. The first was a series of Refresher Courses for Teachers, some of which were devoted to illustrating the latest techniques in lecture demonstration using advanced equipment. Teachers who came responded with enthusiasm, but attendances soon proved inadequate to warrant the amount of effort involved within the RI. One factor influencing this result seems to have been the parallel development of Nuffield Science Teaching Courses which demanded much extra work from teachers and moreover laid emphasis on children conducting their own individual experiments, with a positive bias *away* from demonstrations. The second activity which the Institution organised for science teachers consisted of a series of Research Days. On each occasion some leader of research (one was Sir Eric Rideal after he had retired from the RI) brought members of his team to the RI with apparatus and diagrams. Displays were organised in the Libraries, the leader would talk in the Theatre, and those present would then divide into groups and be conducted round the various 'stations' where they could question individual research workers – an interesting anticipation of what are now commonly known as 'poster sessions'. Though popular with the teachers at first, these Research Days also began to dwindle away. The Association for Science Education was holding specialist meetings, and some local authorities were setting up Science Centres. Science programmes on television were increasing in number, including those run by the Open University. The RI in fact was no longer offering a unique service, and pressure on its available space was intense before the opening of the Bernard Sunley Theatre, of which more anon. Nevertheless efforts such as these do not deserve to be written off as mere failures. In some senses they even illustrate one of the Institution's major strengths, namely the flexibility with which it handles its programmes. Capabilities for imaginative pump-priming are immense within the RI but, once the ideas have begun to catch on generally, the necessarily limited capacities of a single building are better switched into other channels. The same process may well be repeated in the future in connection with some now current activities. Moreover it should in fairness be added that the Institution continues to receive a trickle of individual requests from teachers and others for help and guidance on many of the matters just touched on. Every effort is made to meet and answer all such requests.

While still considering the RI's role in education we are now ready to move from the refinement of direct methods of teaching science and mathematics to young people into the wider sphere of rousing interest, spreading knowledge and keeping touch between disciplines. But first a digression is needed centred round the famous RI courses of Christmas Lectures which (as already pointed out in Chapter 8) are half way between these two spheres and really belong to both. The Christmas Lectures appeal to the young of all ages, and their popularity and often lasting influence depend not so much upon the direct instruction given as upon the interest aroused, the insight and inspiration imparted. Their success with the audiences which pack the Theatre year by year continues much as it has ever done since Faraday started the series, but their reputation is now being spread more widely in two very different ways. In the first place, sets of lectures closely based on our Christmas Lectures have been organised in centres outside London, starting with Liverpool and Manchester and now extended to the North-East and to Scotland. But far more important has been the growth of the practice of televising and broadcasting all six RI Christmas Lectures, so that they can be savoured not only in the Theatre itself but also throughout Britain – a practice which began in 1966, after negotiations started by Porter even while still at Sheffield and brought to successful conclusion as his first major achievement at the RI. These broadcasts have continued annually to date, winning wide renown. The interaction between the RI's educational activities and television has indeed become so prominent that it deserves special consideration. Television can be used to inspire wonder just as much as to teach facts and methods.

The public broadcasting of television programmes was still in its infancy in Sir William Bragg's time, though one black and white recording of him lecturing still exists in which he says how glad he is to be able to address his audience through this new medium. Through the fifties and sixties W.L. Bragg and the RI staff worked hard with the BBC to develop the technical skills needed to improve the televised image of a lecture while at the same time avoiding distractions which break the continuity and impact of what is going on inside the lecture room itself (some ludicrous early mishaps have already been described). Early educational broadcasts or films taken in the RI were mainly of lectures specially organised for that purpose. A few Friday Discourses were broadcast, but this practice was discontinued, partly because the BBC did not look kindly on single lectures which lasted a full hour on television. Real success had to wait until the complete course of Christmas Lectures could be broadcast.

All these scientific lectures naturally depend for success upon the lecturer's logical arrangement, clarity of delivery, and capacity to maintain contact with the audience. A great tradition has been built up at the RI that scientific demonstrations should be as simple as possible, each point being made not so much by description as by seeing the half-expected result actually take shape. Demonstrations of that kind must not fail, and success depends not only on the lecturer, but just as much upon the marshalling of experiments and the availability of suitable equipment. In this sphere the RI has established a reputation which is second to none. Partly this has been due to the ever increasing stores of equipment used in historic experiments carried out in the RI since the early years of last century, and available when required for demonstrations or even for re-use – as when the Queen standing in the main Lecture Theatre used Faraday's famous anchor ring (and Davy's battery) to activate the electric current which re-opened his laboratory in the basement. But more important than equipment itself has been the accumulated understanding of how to use it to best advantage. Such understanding has been built up in many teaching laboratories, but at the RI it is more multidisciplinary than is usual elsewhere. Many are the subjects on which Discourses have been and are being given, and the experimental staff cannot foretell what kind of new problem they may not be asked to solve. W.A. Coates, the Senior Experimental Officer, has even been required to dress up as a gorilla and enter into competition with a live chimpanzee! The very varied expertise thus developed makes use indeed of past traditions, and can produce teak-topped tables on which to repeat historic experiments with the original equipment; but the staff are also supplied with the latest visual and other aids, and are supported by a workshop on the premises capable of improvising adaptations or making new equipment.

Such demonstrations cannot be made successful without much effort, and until not so long ago the main effort was aimed at improving the quality of the education and enlightenment provided for those who came to watch and listen in Albemarle Street. Latterly however the greater thrust has been towards spreading the influence of all this expertise beyond the limits of a single building. This has been done in two main ways. Efforts were at first concentrated upon the Science Seminars already described, by providing the equipment needed for demonstrations in the local laboratories to which pupils on each course dispersed after spending their first day at the RI; and also, where necessary, by advising the local lecturing staff on methods of demonstration. The increasing popularity and multiplication of these Science Seminars has however raised problems of how to avoid overstretching the capabilities of the small RI staff. Occasional excursions have also been made with the aim of spreading the message still further afield, and Coates has assisted in the demonstration of RI equipment as far away as Sydney, NSW, and Chicago.

The RI's efforts to improve the quality of filmed and televised versions of scientific lectures have attracted increasing appreciation in many spheres. As well as encouraging the making of films (such as the Millbank series sponsored by ICI and released through their Film Service) the Institution collaborated in 1971 and 1972 with London Weekend Television in the production of two successful science programmes. Most of the progressive development of skills has however been achieved in collaboration with the BBC which has adopted the policy of making as few personal changes as possible in the team which is sent annually to the RI, with the result that the technicians from both sides meet again as friends eager for maximum co-operation. Not only do many helpful suggestions come from the Institution staff, but it is also often agreed that special equipment can best be built in Albemarle Street, thus avoiding delays and limitations imposed by the red tape inevitable in an organisation as large as the BBC. In the early years many breaks and retakes were necessary before an acceptable film could be achieved. Now the standards reached in recording Christmas Lectures have risen to remarkably high levels. Not only can three or four large cameras be operated effectively without disturbing the continuity of the lectures being given to packed audiences in the Theatre; interest there is actually increased. As a trolley is wheeled forward and the camera on it sweeps round to focus on a new experiment, the attention of the audience sweeps with it. Often several cameras point at the same experiment, and both experts and uninitiated can enjoy the unobtrusive way in which they operate without breaking the flow of the lecturer's exposition: indeed the monitoring screens often give clearer views of what is going on than any particular member of the audience can see from his seat. In order to produce such convincing and seemingly simple results on television the whole of each of the six lectures has to be gone through in the Theatre three times.

R I activities connected with television are not confined to the Christmas Lectures. To quote some other examples, the Institution helped to mount a series of scientific debates called 'Controversy' televised in the main R I Lecture Theatre from 1971 to 1975, generally with the Director in the chair. A series of BBC Current Affairs debates organised on similar lines was recorded in 1977. The R I also provided apparatus for a BBC programme on Madame Curie and trained the non-scientific actress to perform her historic experiments perfectly. The popular series of programmes called 'Young Scientist of the Year' which the BBC ran annually on TV from 1970 to 1982 grew out of the 'Science Fair' sponsored by the *Sunday Times* in which George Porter had taken part since 1966. From 1976 these programmes culminated in the presentation of the Royal Institution Trophy by our Director. There has also been frequent collaboration in the production of Open University programmes, especially in the 1982 programmes on photochemistry in which Porter and other members of the laboratory took prominent parts – one section of this received the Royal Society of Chemistry Film and Video award for 1983. In Open University programmes a special effort is made to find the right balance between science, education and entertainment, and in a discourse given in March 1984 Dr Crilly, the BBC executive producer, paid tribute to the lessons which had been learnt both from precedents and from current expertise in the Royal Institution. Finally the R I has recently (1984) decided to extend its activities beyond the realm of television into that of video tapes. Arrangements have been made jointly with two other bodies for the production and sale of video tapes of past series of Christmas Lectures.

Such technicalities are so crucial to the continued vitality of the R I that they have deserved a considerable digression. We must return now to mention other recent efforts by the Institution to interest and inspire all listeners in all disciplines. The effectiveness of such initiatives aimed at attracting people in search of knowledge into the building was greatly helped by the creation of the Bernard Sunley Lecture Theatre in which a hundred persons can now meet together for discussions or demonstrations in an atmosphere of comfort and intimacy. This project had been suggested in W.L Bragg's time but no money was available. A passage and the under-used remnants of the old Model Room were finally opened up as a smaller theatre in 1970. Another great attraction was provided by the refurbishing of Michael Faraday's Laboratory in the basement, re-created with meticulous accuracy and arranged so that its contents can be inspected safely by the public. A new Museum was formed at the same time alongside, where historical apparatus from all stages of the Institution's development is exhibited and explained in simple terms. To stand in the very place where Faraday worked and to see all around his original equipment and experiments has brought home to many people the true flavour of what went on in that historic basement. Close by, an Archives department (now run as an integral part of the Library organisation) has been created in vaults and rooms which had previously been dark, mouldering and neglected. Rare books, manuscripts and other records are now stored and consulted there in healthy and attractive conditions. The official opening of all these basement rooms by the Queen accompanied by the Duke of Edinburgh in February 1973 was a landmark for all concerned with the RI, the first time that our Patron, the reigning monarch, had ever entered the building.

It is perhaps in the Library that it is easiest for the outside world to meet and benefit from the spirit of willing helpfulness which permeates the whole Institution so characteristically, for the Librarian also holds the official status of Information Officer and more than half the questions which she answers come from outside the membership. Despite the limits of accommodation and a tiny staff, the Library and Archives taken together can provide a veritable Aladdin's Cave of unexpected wonders for persons of very varying tastes – this can be true for the most serious of historical researchers, for amateurs trying to glimpse the drift of some other discipline with which they are un-acquainted, and even for youngsters looking avidly for books on science fiction. The RI believes that its educational mission includes a duty to provide as much help as possible for those who search for knowledge and understanding. The Library tries to include non-specialist books on every branch of science, and new areas of coverage are added as they become prominent – recent examples being environmental problems, also nuclear and solar energy. It includes books which scientists have written on non-scientific subjects, which brings in science and religion as well as many other topics. In addition it endeavours to provide the specialist literature required by every researcher in the DF laboratory, also in the Science History organisation of which more anon. Books are being slowly re-arranged by subject matter so that they can be found more easily by the non-specialist: the new Junior Section has stimulated much interest among the young. To help make room for new purchases (over 300 books are now bought each year) there is a steady policy of selling books thought to have become outmoded, but this only applies to books known to remain available elsewhere, as for example back numbers of many periodicals. When asked for books it does not possess, the RI tries (through its close contacts with other libraries) either to obtain loaned copies or to provide information as to where they can be found. Some RI books are let out to Members on loan.

The Institution has long been interested in the development of active research into the History of Science, and a Reader in this subject was appointed in 1970. The completion of the new archive rooms added greatly to the facilities available for studying and cataloguing memorabilia stored away in the building and a promotion group was formed of Members having suitable technical experience. In 1982 a new formal structure was set up entitled The Royal Institution Centre for the History of Science and Technology (RICHST). Research Fellows are appointed, papers have been published, and a number of interesting seminars have been held and are being planned.

A considerable number of Circles or Discussion Groups have been organised during the last twenty years, varying in size and in frequency of meetings. Some have been confined to Members of the Institution, meeting together under the guidance of some expert; whereas others have welcomed persons from outside. Groups vary in character, some having precise academic aims while others spread widely over general cultural interests. The Library Circle was one of the earliest and reports of many of its meetings make interesting reading. In 1977 it changed its name into the Library Discussion Group. The Photochemistry Discussion Group has close links with the DF Laboratory and is therefore always active. The History of Science Group tended from an early stage to concentrate upon studying a single subject through a number of meetings, and eventually evolved into being one aspect of the new organisation RICHST mentioned in the last paragraph. It has not always been easy to find the right format which would crystallise initial enthusiasms sufficiently to maintain a lively group membership, and there has been a noticeable tendency to replace frequent lunch-time meetings by more widely spaced colloquia, each lasting half or a whole day. An Education Discussion Group was very active for several years, but was discontinued after 1980. Regrets were expressed when the

Young Members Group, which had started so hopefully in 1970, had to be wound up because of small attendance at meetings, possibly influenced by the increasing cost of travelling into London in the evenings.

Efforts to further education and mutual understanding have been spread on a much wider scale by special conferences, expositions, colloquia, symposia and fora (how many other names can one invent to describe such activities?) organised by the Royal Institution usually with the help of generous sponsors. There have been too many for detailed mention here, but they have aimed at spreading information through industrial, international and governmental circles, several being addressed or chaired by cabinet ministers. Titles have included Industrial Technologies (1975), International Symposium on Lasers in Chemistry (1977), Nuclear Power and the Energy Future (1977), and Third World Strategies and the Role of Industrial Countries (1979). Each has aimed at a special objective, but they have all had the subsidiary effect of spreading appreciation of the RI's attractions among wider circles, and a number of new Members have been introduced through these various sources.

It is time now to consider social and club activities, to provide which is the third main aspect of the Institution's objectives; and we should remember that from its very start the RI has developed in and around the gentleman's private house which the infant Institution bought in 1799. That house can still be visualised in the stately divided staircase leading up to the first floor and in the door marked 'Servants Hall' that leads into Faraday's laboratory. However much this building has been altered to meet growing needs, it is truly of scientific and historical importance, and the Institution and its Members are responsible for maintaining and adapting it, and receive no grants for such purposes. Much more than mere routine maintenance has been needed recently. Major improvements have been achieved like the Bernard Sunley Theatre and the Faraday Museum and Archives Department already mentioned, and in 1967 a suite of DF laboratories was reconstructed to make them suitable for Professor Porter's new team of chemists. Alterations have been needed not only in the original Institution building, 21 Albemarle Street, but also in the three houses to the south of it. Complicated changes have been effected in both Numbers 20 and 19 after the termination of various sub-leases – with results which are at present reminiscent of a rabbit warren even though the Institution has thereby gained much-needed additional accommodation. The next house, Number 18, was purchased just at the time when Porter succeeded Bragg. This was regarded chiefly as an investment, but the RI has since moved into the basement. Moreover electrical services have been renewed by stages throughout about half the block, no mean achievement in buildings containing so many research laboratories.

A recent expansion has brought to light a nice story. The RI has taken over the basement of Number 20, which includes a series of strongrooms previously occupied by Cartiers. We have now been told that these strongrooms were constructed during the last war for General de Gaulle who needed storage for the central funds of the Free French.

Within the structures thus carefully refurbished, strenuous efforts have been made to provide functions and facilities which old and new Members find attractive today, traditions and innovations being scrupulously balanced. Routine social activities remain centred round the evenings when Discourses are given – after a brief trial of Thursdays for a few summers these have now reverted to Friday evenings during what may be thought of as being roughly equivalent to the three university terms. Average attendance has increased in recent years to the present figure of about 400. Formal dress (now black tie) is still worn by most, though not all; and it is worth noting that this custom was overwhelmingly endorsed by a referendum of Members in 1967. Before the lecture a bar is opened in the Council Room (known until recently as the Managers' Room) and Members and their guests also cluster together in the four public reception rooms on the first floor, in three of which coffee, tea and cakes are served after the lecture (no refreshments are allowed into the Main Library). Increasing emphasis has been given to the exhibitions in the Library arranged by the Librarian to suit that particular Discourse. The Director, with Lady Porter's graceful support, has continued and developed the practice (revived by W.H. Bragg with the support of *his* wife now commemorated by a bas-relief in the Entrance Hall) of holding a formal dinner party before the lecture, and later of inviting selected guests to drinks in the Director's flat. The Porters also hold formal receptions.

Further social activities are arranged for members of most of the Discussion Groups already mentioned in connection with Education. Parties take place and visits are organised both for the groups individually and for such Members generally as may wish to participate. From time to time there are also major Institution events attended by royalty and other distinguished guests, including for example the Faraday Centenary (1967), the Bragg Symposium (1970), the opening of the Faraday Laboratory and Museum by the Queen (1973 as already mentioned), the Silver Jubilee Party (1977), and the Davy Bicentenary Celebration in 1978. The Institution provides a fine setting for great occasions of this kind; it is at the same time stately and friendly, and this combination adds greatly to the enjoyment of those who participate. To attend an RI party is fun; one hears this said so often with shining eyes. The writers of this book are well placed to know how true it is, for (as well as attending functions as Members) we were allowed to hold our own wedding reception in the RI and, since years later two nieces also had their wedding parties there, we could gauge the success of such occasions from both sides. What is more, we were even told that a commercial catering manager had exclaimed what an ideal place the Institution is for a large family wedding – he wished it could be available for hire!

All these activities could not have been realised without the intro-duction of two radical changes. The first was in the administrative and constitutional basis upon which the Institution had been run. The organisation inherited from the past involved several types of in-efficiency, but earlier attempts to change it had created even more difficulties. Consideration of how best to achieve efficient reform started anew in 1966 and proceeded systematically, taking care at every stage to secure overwhelming approval from all concerned. New basic principles had been agreed on administrative matters by the end of 1967, laying down the division of responsibilities between, on the one hand, the Honorary Officers who are elected by the Members and, on the other, the Director who was also appointed Executive Secretary with freshly defined authorities in staff matters. But more fundamental aspects could not be changed so easily, being controlled by Acts of Parliament, the Privy Council and the Charity Commission. A com-plicated revision of the constitution was eventually agreed by all concerned from Members of the RI up to the Privy Council, the most obvious change being the amalgamation of the separate Committees of Managers and Visitors into a single Council, supported by Standing Committees and an independent Audits Committee. After inevitable delays this finally took effect in 1984.

The second radical change needed was in financial management, particularly including fund raising. That the RI needed a larger income had become painfully obvious long before currency inflation began to pose a serious threat. Grants had been forthcoming for decades towards research in the DF, and W.L. Bragg had secured donations from Industry and Commerce towards the Schools Lectures: but no support was available for general activities within the Institution itself. WLB had made a useful start on plugging this hole by creating the new membership class of Corporate Subscribers, whose payments soon rivalled those by ordinary Members; but much more was still needed. Two public appeals were launched with considerable success, the Faraday Centenary Appeal in 1967 and a second in 1976, both evoking generous responses. Moreover a way was found to raise more cash from the membership without imposing too heavy burdens upon them. Since 1973 Members have had to pay for seats occupied by themselves or their guests at Discourses and other important events. This ended the somewhat unseemly competition for seats which occurred on over-crowded evenings before seat reservation was introduced, even though the number of Members and Associates had doubled between 1966 and 1983. The cost of tickets has been kept far below what must be expected for most entertainments in London, yet it has thereby become possible to avoid crippling increases in annual subscriptions. It is moreover interesting to note that this change seems to have increased the average number of attendances. Some Members hesitate before bringing guests to after-dinner lectures when they have no certainty of obtaining seats.

A further financial development took place in 1982 which also carries important implications for future co-operation in scientific education throughout the country, enabling forward planning to be started with greater hopes of success. The Department of Education and Science acting through the Royal Society started making annual grants to the RI towards the cost of the Schools Lectures and for innovation and experiment in the educational field. These grants were promised initially for five and three years respectively and have since been increased. Repeated earlier efforts to obtain such official grants had all foundered, partly it appears because of lingering uncertainties regarding the relative roles of the Royal Institution, the British Association and other scientific bodies; there was an understandable desire not to encourage any latent atmosphere of competition. In 1981 however a joint committee was set up under the chairmanship of Sir Andrew Huxley as President of the Royal Society. This clarified the position to the satisfaction of all parties, with agreement that no overlap is involved; and this committee's conclusions sufficed to remove the last governmental hesitation regarding payment of grant. Though these grants of public funds are modest, they will strengthen the RI's abilities to develop innovations in the field of education. Lest this last comment be misunderstood, the reader should be reminded here of earlier statements that research at the RI has managed to remain self-supporting throughout recent decades thanks to grants raised by and given to the research team itself from Industry and particularly from the Science and Engineering Research Council.

It is time now to draw together the three main threads, and to attempt some assessment of the Institution's present health and future prospects. However tentative such an attempt may be, this is a good moment at which to make it. We are not much more than ten years away from the date when preparations will begin for the Institution's bicentenary and a very thorough review is likely to be made then. It seems possible that judgements (and even misjudgements) made here might help to stimulate and clarify the thought which will be needed in the coming decade.

What are the RI's main assets and resources?

The first asset is a very practical one, namely the site and buildings. We have already spoken about the buildings, but great importance should also be attached to the possession of such a site in central London (on a ground lease which is supposed to be due to expire in the year 3921!). Both the writers of this book know from personal experience that living in Albemarle Street can have its domestic disadvantages – particularly on airless afternoons in a hot summer when Green Park is the nearest place where one can be happy to push a pram. But for an institution the position is ideal: it is easily accessible both for members and for visiting academics (more than ever so since the Victoria and Jubilee tubes have been running), and street parking does not present insuperable problems in the evenings when Discourses are given. The financial advantages of this site are moreover likely to increase when outmoded leases of adjoining premises expire; some leases of property sub-let by the RI are of very long standing.

The second asset is vaguer, but no less potent for that. It starts with the RI's reputation for having maintained continuously through two centuries the power to interest in each other's new discoveries the minds and tastes of persons attached to widely different philosophies. Gwendy Caroe put it more vividly:

Although the old 18th-century ideal of comprehensive knowledge is now quite unrealisable, the RI has kept on an ideal of interest in all knowledge, of knowing at least what different subjects are about; a touch of hands, a link of understanding.

The RI has managed to keep before us this lively memory of the universality of knowledge by an almost loving blend of tradition, good-will, and skilled direction. The *tradition* needs no further emphasis here. The *goodwill* is enormous, reaching out into so many branches of educated thought and spreading now over an ever widening geo-graphical area. The RI's growing appeal to the younger generation has become self-evident, especially since the category of Junior Associates was established in 1978. That the *direction* has been and still is skilled has I believe been amply demonstrated in these pages. The interests and the activities of successive Resident Professors and Directors have varied in many ways, but all have been able to add something important. The greatest tribute one can pay to the wisdom of past Committees of Managers is to applaud their successes in choosing Resident Professors and Directors. That wisdom will be needed again in the future. The selection of successive Directors is indeed the greatest responsibility which remains with the Managers (recently reconsti-tuted as the Council), now that the more important initiatives in the control of current activities have in the interests of efficiency been conceded to the Director in office.

The third asset may be summarised as the reservoir of equipment and skilled personnel which has been established at the RI and is still growing. Again there is no need to repeat what has already been written, but there is a gloss which needs adding. In recent years it has become possible to think of the Institution and the Davy–Faraday Laboratory as different aspects of the same unity, but they still need thinking about separately when considering continuity. The Institu-tion itself works characteristically in so many varied fields that such a diversity of activities may reasonably be expected to continue indefinitely, however much the principal centres may change to meet changing needs. The same cannot be said, however, about the Davy–Faraday if past precedents are followed. Since 1923 the central thrust of DF research has usually been linked with that of the current Director, and therein lies one of the chief problems which will face the Council whenever the choice of a new Director is under consideration. The problem is made all the more acute by the high reputation which the Davy–Faraday has established as a place from which one can expect important research to emerge. Moreover this reputation has been sustained in such different ways over such a large part of the present century that it seems no longer reasonable to continue entertaining doubts (such as many people had in the fifties and sixties) as to whether there could be a permanently viable place under modern conditions for a small research laboratory in the heart of London. By now a quarter of a century's progress has shown that the Davy–Faraday Laboratory *is* viable. Today the research team working there is larger than at any time in its history. This strongly suggests that for a long time to come there will remain a need for an independent laboratory which can offer facilities not only to the Director's team but also to visiting professors on sabbatical leave and to younger researchers in need of temporary facilities. This has become particularly clear since the Royal Institution formed close links with several colleges in the University of London, so that students carrying out research at the RI can also be internal students of colleges in the University, an arrangement which works to the benefit of all.

W.L. Bragg wrote that the Royal Institution 'is a national treasure house of a unique kind'. George Porter has called it 'the London Repertory Theatre of Science'. It might equally be thought of as a forcing bed for the propagation of new ideas in experimentation, discovery and education. This chapter has only touched on some of the Institution's activities during the last two decades, yet it has suggested many just grounds for pride: but that which remains foremost in the mind is pride in the combination of tradition and flexibility which has become part of the RI's way of life. Both are likely to be needed as much as ever in this modern world of nuclear experiments, microchips, computers and democracy. Perhaps the most fitting way to end this summary of a past which holds out great promise for the future is to quote another of the *obiter dicta* which Gwendy Caroe left behind:

The ideals and the life will go on in the RI, sometimes halting like water poured on to the sands, but always finding a new way towards the sea. One of the many streams in the world, it is wriggling its way to Truth – perhaps truth is too big a word: let us say to Understanding. I salute the Royal Institution with reverence and affection.

Some Sources

Andrade, E.N. da C. 'William Henry Bragg 1862–1942', in *Obit. Not. Fellows Roy. Soc. 4*, 1943, 277–300.

Armstrong, H.E. *James Dewar 1842–1923: A Friday Evening Lecture to the Members of the Royal Institution on 18 January, 1924*, London, Benn, 1924.

Armstrong, H.E. *Low-Temperature Research at the Royal Institution of Great Britain London 1900–1907*. London, Clowes, 1909.

Babbage, C. *Reflections on the Decline of Science in England, and on Some of its Causes*, London, Fellowes, 1830.

Becker, B.H. *Scientific London*, London, King, 1874.

Bence-Jones, M. 'Science in London's West End – The Royal Institution', in *Country Life*, 2 Sept. 1965, 544–546.

Bibby, C. *T.H. Huxley; Scientist, Humanist and Educator*, London, Watts, 1959.

Blake, A. et al. *Great Chefs of France*, London, Mitchell Beazley, 1978.

Bragg, W.H. 'History in the Archives of the Royal Society', in *Nature, 144*, 1939, 21–28.

Bragg, W.H. *Michael Faraday*, London, BBC, 1931.

Bragg, W. Lawrence. *Science and Adventure of Living*, London, British Association for the Advancement of Science, 1930.

Bragg, W. Lawrence. 'The Development of X-Ray Analysis. The Rutherford Memorial Lecture delivered at Christchurch, New Zealand, 1960', in *Roy. Soc. Proc. 262A*, 1961, 145–158.

Bragg, W. Lawrence. 'the difference between living and non-living matter from a physical point of view', in *Science and Culture, 30*, 1964, 161–167.

Bragg, W. Lawrence. 'Between two Cultures: Encouraging the Young', in *The Times*, 31 Oct., 1963, p.13.

Bragg, W. Lawrence. 'The Art of Talking About Science', in *Science, 154*, 1966, 1613–1616.

Bragg, W. Lawrence. 'The Spirit of the Science', in *The Listener, 31*, 1944, 147–8 and in *Proc. R. Soc. Edinb., A67*, 1967, 303–308.

Bragg, W. Lawrence. 'What Makes a Scientist?' Lecture for Civil Servants in *Proc. R.I., 42*, 1968, 397–410.

Bragg, W. Lawrence. *The Development of X-Ray Analysis*, edited by D. Phillips. London, Bell, 1975.

Brock, W.H. ed. et al. *The Journals of Thomas Archer Hirst* (Microfiche). London, Mansell, 1980.

Brown, S.C. *Benjamin Thompson, Count Rumford*, London, MIT Press, 1979.

Cannon, S.F. *Science in Culture: the Early Victorian Period*, London, Dawson, 1978.

Caroe, A.D.R. *The House of the Royal Institution*, London, 1963.

Caroe, G.M. 'The Royal Institution in Sir William Bragg's time', in *Proc. R.I., 40*, 1965, 398–416.

Caroe, G.M. *W.H. Bragg: Man and Scientist*. Cambridge, University Press, 1979.

Caroe, G.M. & W.L. Bragg. 'Sir William Bragg, FRS (1862–1942)', in *Notes and Records of the Royal Society 17 (2)*, 1962, 169–182.

Carrier, E.O. *Humphry Davy and Chemical Discovery*, London, Chatto, 1967.

Chancellor, J. *Charles Darwin*, London, Weidenfeld & Nicolson, 1973.

Cory, R. 'Fifty years at the Royal Institution', in *Proc. R.I.*, *34*, 1947–1950, 661–673.

Cornwell, J. *Coleridge: Poet and Revolutionary 1772–1804*, London, Longman, 1973.

Crosse, C.A.H. *Science and Society in the Fifties*, N.P. 1891.

Davidoff, L. *Best Circles: Society, the Season & Etiquette*, London, Croom Helm, 1973.

Davy, J. *Memoirs of the Life of Sir Humphry Davy*, London, Longman, 1836.

Edgeworth, M. *The Life & Letters of Maria Edgeworth*, London, Arnold, 1984.

Eve, A.S. & Creasy, C.H. *Life and Work of John Tyndall*, London, Macmillan, 1945.

Faraday, M. *Commonplace Book*, Vol 2. Holograph including journal of continental journey, lodged in the Royal Institution Library.

Faraday, M. *Faraday's Diary, being the various philosophical notes of experimental investigation, 1820–1862*, edited by T. Martin, London, Bell, 1932.

Faraday, M. & Bragg, W.L. *Advice to Lecturers. An anthology taken from the Writings of Michael Faraday and Lawrence Bragg*, London, Mansell for the Royal Institution, 1974.

Foote, G.A. 'Sir Humphry Davy and his Audience at the Royal Institution', in *Isis, 43*, 1952, 6–12.

Forgan, S. *The Royal Institution of Great Britain 1840–1873*. Thesis, University of London, unpublished.

Forgan, S. ed. *Science and the Sons of Genius. Papers presented at the Bicentenary Symposium*, London, Science Reviews, 1980.

Forster, E.M. *Marianne Thornton: A Domestic Biography (1797–1887)*, London, Arnold, 1956.

Fox, C. *The Journals of Caroline Fox, 1835–1871*, edited by W. Monk, London, Elek, 1972.

Geikie, A. *Memoir of Sir Andrew Crombie Ramsay*, London, Macmillan, 1895.

Gladstone, J. *Michael Faraday*, London, Macmillan, 1872.

Green, W. 'Some memories of the Royal Institution and its Laboratories 1900–1950', in *Proc. R.I. 36*, 1955–57, 543–567.

Hall, A.R. 'The Royal Society of Arts: Two Centuries of Progress in Science and Technology', in *J. R. Soc. Arts, 122*, 1974, 641–658.

Harrison, J.F.C. *A History of the Working Men's College 1854–1954*, London, Routledge, 1954.

Hartley, H. *Humphry Davy*, London, Nelson, 1966.

Hawthorne, N. *Our Old Home: a series of English sketches* (vol 5 of the Centenary Edition) Athens, Ohio, University Press, 1970.

Healey, E. *Lady Unknown – The Life of Angela Burdett-Coutts*, London, Sidgwick & Jackson, 1978.

Holdsworth, W. *History of English Law*, Vol 10 (Historical Background), London, Methuen, 1956–66.

Holland, E. *Journal, 1791–1811*, edited by the Earl of Ilchester, London, Longmans, 1908.

Holland, H. *Recollections of Past Life*, London, Longmans, 1872.

Holland S. *A Memoir of the Reverend Sydney Smith*, London, Longmans, 1855.

Hudson, D. *Munby, Man of Two Worlds*, London, Murray, 1972.

Humboldt, F.H.A., von. *Personal narrative of Travels to the Equinoctial Regions of the New Continent During the Years 1799–1804*, London, Longman, 1814–1826.

Huxley, T. *Collected Essays*, London, Macmillan, 1893–4.

Ironmonger, E. 'The Royal Institution and the Teaching of Science in the Nineteenth Century', in *Proc. R.I. 37*, 1958, 139–158.

Jones, H.B. *Report on the past, present and future of the Royal Institution chiefly in regard to its encouragement of Scientific Research*, London, Clowes, 1862.

Jones, H.B. *The Life and Letters of Faraday*, London, Longmans, 1870.

Jones, H.B. *The Royal Institution: Its Founder and Its First Professors*, London, Longmans, 1871.

King, R. *Michael Faraday of the Royal Institution*, London, Royal Institution, 1973.

King, R. *Humphry Davy*, London, Royal Institution, 1978.

Lankester, E.R. *Science and Education*, [seven lectures delivered at the Royal Institution in 1854 by W. Whewell, M .Faraday, R.G. Latham, G.G.B. Daubeny, J. Tyndall, J. Paget and W.B. Hodgson ('7 Great Guns')], London, Heinemann, 1917.

Martin, T. *The Royal Institution*, London, Longmans, 1948.

Milton, J. 'Lectures and Lecturers in the first 100 Years of the Royal Institution', in *Proc. R.I., 50*, 1978, 133–144.

Moll, G. *On the alleged decline of Science in England, by a Foreigner*, edited by Michael Faraday, London, Boosey, 1831.

Paris, J.A. *The Life of Sir Humphry Davy*, London, Colburn, 1831.

Phillips, D. 'William Lawrence Bragg 31 March 1890 – 1 July 1971', in *Biog. Mem. of Fellows of the Roy. Soc., 25*, 1979, 75–143.

Plumb, J.H. *England in the Eighteenth Century*, London, Penguin, 1969.

Pollock, W.F. *Personal Remembrances of Sir Frederick Pollock*, London, Macmillan, 1887.

Porter, G. 'The Royal Institution – Its History and Future' in *New Scientist*, 29 Sept, 1977, 802–804.

Porter, G. 'Quick as a Flash', in *Proc. R.I., 42*, 1968–69, 193–213.

Rayleigh, R.J.S., 4th Baron. 'Some Reminiscences of Scientific Workers of the Past Generation, and their Surroundings', in *Proc. Phys. Soc. 48*, 1936, 217–46.

Richardson, J. *Pre-eminent Victorian: Study of Tennyson*, London, Greenwood, 1962.

Roderick, G.W. *Scientific and Technical Education in Nineteenth-Century England*, Newton Abbott, David and Charles, 1972.

Roscoe, H. *The Life and Experience of Sir Henry Enfield Roscoe, Written by Himself*, London, Macmillan, 1906.

Royal Institution, London. *The Archives of the Royal Institution of Great Britain in facsimile. Minutes of Managers' Meetings 1799–1903*, edited by F. Greenaway, London, Scolar Press, 1971.

Sharrock, R. 'The Chemist and the Poet: Sir Humphry Davy and the Preface to "Lyrical Ballads" ', in *Notes Roy. Soc. Lond. 17*, 1962, 57–76.

Smiles, S. *Self help: With Illustrations of Character and Conduct*, London, Murray, 1860.

Smith, A.G.R. *Science and Society in the Sixteenth and Seventeenth Centuries*, London, Thames and Hudson, 1972.

Thomson, D. *England in the Nineteenth Century*, London, Penguin, 1970.

Toulmin, S., *The Discovery of Time*, London, Hutchinson, 1965.

Trevelyan, G.M. *English Social History*, London, Penguin, 1970.

Trevelyan, R. *Pre-Raphaelite Circle*, London, Chatto, 1978.

Turner, G.L'E. *The Patronage of Science in the Nineteenth Century*, Leyden, Noordhoff, 1976.

Tyndall, J. *New Fragments of Science*, London, Longmans, 1892.

Vernon, K. 'The Foundation and Early Years of the Royal Institution', in *Proc. R.I. 39*, 1962, 364–402.

Watson, J. *The Double Helix*, London, Weidenfeld & Nicolson, 1968.

Watts, I. *The Improvement of the Mind*, London, 1809.

Willey, B. *Eighteenth-Century Background*, London, Chatto, 1946.

Winstanley, D.A. *Unreformed Cambridge. A Study of Certain Aspects of the University in the Eighteenth Century*, Cambridge, University Press, 1935.

Williams, L.P. *Michael Faraday: A Biography*, London, Chapman, 1965.

Williams, L.P. *The Selected Correspondence of Michael Faraday*, London, Cambridge University Press, 1971.

Whewell, W. *The philosophy of the inductive sciences founded upon their history*, London, Parker, 1840.

Suggestions for Further Reading

Andrade, E.N. da C. *A Brief History of the Royal Society 1660–1960*, London, Royal Society, 1960.

Baker, E.C. *Sir William Preece, F.R.S. Victorian Engineer Extraordinary*, London, Hutchinson, 1976.

Brock, W. ed. et al. *John Tyndall. Essays on a Natural Philosopher*, Dublin, Royal Dublin Society, 1981.

Cottrell, A. 'Edward Neville da Costa Andrade 1887–1971', in *Biographical Memoirs of Fellows of the Royal Society, 18*, 1972, 1–20.

Crowther, J.G. *Scientific Types*, London, Barrie & Rockliff, 1968.

Eley, D.D. 'Eric Keightley Rideal 1890–1974', in *Biographical Memoirs of Fellows of the Royal Society, 22*, 1976, 381–413.

Feldberg, W.S. 'Henry Hallett Dale 1875–1968', in *Biographical Memoirs of Fellows of the Royal Society, 16*, 1970, 77–174.

Gooding, D. ed. et al. *Faraday Rediscovered. Essays on the Life and work of Michael Faraday 1791–1857*, London, Macmillan, 1985.

James, F.A.J.L. ed. *Chemistry and Theology in mid-Victorian London: The Diary of Herbert McLeod 1850–1870*. London, Macmillan, 1986.

Jenkin, J. *The Bragg Family in Adelaide: a pictorial celebration*. Adelaide: La Trobe University, 1986.

Knoepfmacher, U.C. ed. et al. *Nature and the Victorian Imagination*, Berkeley, University of California Press, 1977.

Lodge, O. *Past Years – An Autobiography*, London, Hodder & Stoughton, 1931.

Rayleigh, Fourth Baron (Robert John Strutt). *John William Strutt, Third Baron Rayleigh*, London, Arnold, 1924.

Rayleigh, Fourth Baron. *The Life of Sir J.J. Thomson*, Cambridge, University Press, 1942.

Russell, C.A. ed. *Recent developments in the History of Chemistry*, London, Royal Society of Chemistry, 1985.

Russell, C.A. *Science and Social Change 1700–1900*, London, Macmillan, 1983.

Thompson, J.S. et al. *Silvanus Phillips Thompson, His Life and Letters*, London, Unwin, 1920.

Thompson, S.P. *Michael Faraday*, London, Cassell, 1901.

Tolstoy, I. *James Clerk Maxwell, a biography*, Edinburgh, Canongate, 1981.

Index